Humfrey, Duke of Gloucester

by Ambrose Philips

1723

A FACSIMILE PUBLISHED BY CORNMARKET PRESS
FROM THE COPY IN THE BIRMINGHAM SHAKESPEARE LIBRARY
LONDON
1969

PUBLISHED BY CORNMARKET PRESS LIMITED
42/43 CONDUIT STREET LONDON W1R ONL
PRINTED IN ENGLAND BY FLETCHER AND SON LIMITED NORWICH

SBN 7191 0138 7

HUMFREY,

DUKE of

GLOUCESTER.

A

TRAGEDY.

As it is Acted at the

THEATRE-ROYAL

IN

DRURY-LANE,

BY

His MAJESTY's SERVANTS.

By Mr. PHILIPS.

LONDON,

Printed: And Sold by *J. Roberts* Near the *Oxford-Arms* in *Warwick Lane* 1723.

S I R,

HEN your unwearied Application to the weighty Concerns of the Publick, will allow you the Leifure to perufe this Tragedy; I am perfwaded, the Choice of the Argument will meet with your Approbation : Since, there is not, in *Englifh* Hiftory, any remarkable Event, proper for the Stage, that furnifhes a

A   fairer

DEDICATION.

fairer Occasion of Inculcating those Principles, which tend to the Service of the King, and the Welfare of the Nation. And, notwithstanding your Discernment in Performances of this Kind, may deterr the ablest of our Writers; yet (beside your natural Candour) the Love of your Countrey will incline you to indulge the Inabilities of the Poet, for the Honesty of his Intentions.

The Duke of GLOUCESTER was a Man of Singular Goodness; a wise and upright Statesman; a great Opposer of the oppressive Usurpations of the See of *Rome*; a generous Favourer of the, then, poor and distrest Commons; a powerful Oratour; a most loyal Subject; a learned Prince; and an Encourager of Learning: Which shining Qualities, even without the Advantage of his Birth, would render his Memory dear to You.

It is the Happiness of *England*, that, in the Age wherein You flourish, the Nobles

DEDICATION.

Nobles enjoy all their valuable Privileges ; and yet, the Commons are, neither Poor, nor Diftreft : Whereby, Liberty and Property are become univerfal, in *Great Britain* ; the Government acquires a double Support ; and every Reprefentative of the People has yearly Opportunities to diftinguifh Himfelf as a Patriot.

It is a great Satisfaction to All, who know the Value of a Free Government, to fee, at the Head of a Committee appointed to enquire into the prefent Confpiracy, a Commoner, who is placed above all Hopes and Fears, but thofe, which regard his Countrey : A Gentleman, whofe Abilities, whofe Integrity , whofe unvarying Conduct, whofe Refolution, and whofe ample Circumftances, confpire to make him equal to fo great a Truft.

You, S I R, can approve, or difapprove, of Meafures relating to the Publick ; can accept, or refufe, Employments of Dignity ; influenced by

no

DEDICATION.

no Motive, but the General Good.
This State of Independency (the Bul-
wark of Publick Vertue) has allways
given your Opinions their due Weight,
with equitable Minds. Such an *Eng-
lishman* was the great and good Duke
HUMFREY, in his Time : And, if
you are pleased to countenance my
Endeavours to revive his Fame ; I
shall (with the utmost Gratitude) ac-
knowledge it, as the greatest Honour,
and Obligation.

I am,

With the greatest Respect,

S I R,

Your most Humble, and

most Obedient Servant,

Ambr. Philips.

TO THE
READER.

 **T**HEY, *who have read* Shakespear's *Second Part of* Henry VI. *may, probably, recollect most of the Passages, I have borrowed from Him, either Word for Word, or with some small Alteration.* Nevertheless, *that I may not be thought unwilling to Acknowledge my Obligation to so great a Poet; I desire my Readers will place to his Account, One or Two Hints, and One intire Line, in the* 24th *Page, where* Eleanor's *Penance is related: Four Lines, in the* 38th *Page, where* Beaufort *speaks of* Gloucester's *Popularity: Three Parts in Four of the Description of the Duke's dead Body, in Page* 71: *And about Seventeen Lines in the* last *Scene; some of which are so very beautifull, that it may be questioned, whether there be any Passages, in* Shakespear, *that deserve greater Commendation.*

PROLOGUE;

WRITTEN BY

Mr. *Bartholomew Paman,*

Of the MIDDLE-TEMPLE.

Spoken by Mr. *BOOTH*.

S Education moulds the tender Brain,
Or free, or flavish, Doctrines We maintain.
Where Asia's *Lord, with Power despotick, reigns,*
Whole Nations boast the Privilege of Chains:
Worship some Plant, or Reptile, as a G O D;
And dye with Rapture, at their Tyrant's Nod.
Where never-erring Rome *usurps a Sway,*
To go by Reason, is to go a-stray.
Freedom of Thought, we Britons *justly prize;*
Parent of Liberty, and Scourge of Vice.
In vain, Tradition pleads the Force of Years;
At Reason's Touch, the base Alloy appears.
In foreign Climes, let Monkish Tales preside;
Truth is a Briton's *never-failing Guide.*

Our

PROLOGUE.

Our free-born Bard a free-born Heroe draws :
HUMFREY ; the Patron of Learn'd Wickliff's Cause.
View here, the Force of Bigottry in Kings ;
View here, the Woes, that Superstition brings.
Behold a Statesman, upright, wise, and good ;
Who bravely for his Countrey's Welfare stood :
But, sure Destruction is the Patriot's Doom,
When Kings are Only Ministers of Rome.

In these short Scenes, our Authour has, with Pain,
Sketch'd out the Years of HENRY's troubled Reign ;
Shewn by What Springs vile Politicians move ;
How, Blood and Cruelty, Rome's Prelates love !
Awkward in Plots, They little Cunning show ;
Murder's the deepest Policy they know.

Britons, collect this Moral from our Tale :
Should, once again, the Papal Power prevail ;
Again, Religious Fires would dreadful shine ;
And Inquisitions prove their Right Divine.

The Persons of the Play.

MEN.

Humfrey, Duke of *Gloucester* ; Uncle to the King ; and Lord Protectour of the Realm. } Mr. *Booth.*

His Friends.

Richard Plantagenet ; Duke of *York.*   Mr. *Mills.*
Richard Nevill ; Earl of *Salisbury.*   Mr. *Thurmond.*
Richard Nevill ; Earl of *Warwick* : Son to the Earl of *Salisbury.* } Mr. *Williams.*

Henry Beaufort ; Cardinal, and Bishop of *Winchester* : Uncle to the Duke of *Gloucester* ; and Great-Uncle to the King. } Mr. *Cibber.*

Of His, and the Queen's, Faction.

William de la Pole ; Duke of *Suffolk.*   Mr. *Watson.*
Humfrey Stafford ; Duke of *Buckingham.* Mr. *Mills* jun.

WOMEN.

Margaret, Daughter to *Reiner*, Duke of *Anjou* ; Queen to King *Henry* the Sixth : Secretly in Love with the Duke of *Suffolk.* } Mrs. *Oldfield.*
Eleanor, Dutchess of *Gloucester*, Wife to Duke *Humfrey.* } Mrs. *Porter.*

An Officer of Justice.
Two Ruffians.

The ACTION passes within the King's Palace, in Westminster.

HUMFREY,

DUKE of

GLOUCESTER.

❀❀❀❀❀❀❀❀❀❀❀❀❀❀❀❀❀❀❀❀❀❀❀❀

ACT I. SCENE I.

Duke of York. *Earl of* Salisbury. *Earl of* Warwick.

YORK.

WHY, yes! — my Lords of *Salisbury* and of *Warwick*;
Father and Son, Each of the Other worthy :
It is apparent, *England*'s Glory fades.
Henry of *Bolingbroke* was born for Rule ;
And left a Son, — (O, ever dear Remembrance!)
Whose matchless Vertues prov'd him More than Man. —
But, this Sixth *Henry*.————

B   *Salisb.*

Salisb. Good your Grace of *York* ;——
Forbear to dwell on this unpleafing Theme :——
A King, by Priefts, and by a Woman, govern'd !

   To fave the finking State, be now our Care :
If, happily, We may difpell the Storm,
Black-lowering o'er the Head of noble *Gloucefter* ;
The Safeguard,—— the Protectour, of the Realm.

   My Son, inform us :—— Thou haft feen his High-
      nefs.

   York. Speak, *Warwick* :—— For, on *Gloucefter's* mighty
      Fate,
The doubtfull Welfare of the Land is poiz'd :——
Say, how he bears the Seifure of his Wife ;
This rude Attack, where moft he lies unguarded.

   Warw. Right-Noble *York* ; I need not to unfold
Duke *Humfrey's* Scorn of Slander.—— He contemns
The trivial Malice of his Foes ; and bids
His injur'd Confort, pay their Spight with Smiles ;
Till Time fhall fhew Her loyal, as Himfelf.

   York. Till Time fhall fhew !—— Wherein is
      She Difloyal ?
Moft frivolous Pretence of Guilt !——

   Warw. That, She had fafhion'd
A Model of his Majefty, in Wax ;
With which, his Perfon is to Sympathize ;
Confuming daily, as the Wax confumes.

   York. Now, by my Hopes of Heaven, I could not
      brooke
Such Forgeries againft my Bofome's Darling !——
Such feign'd Offences, as exceed all Faith ;
And bid Defiance to Man's Underftanding.

   Salisb. Urged, like *Plantagenet* !—— The Lord
      Protectour
Too tamely bears this Infult on his Dutchefs.

   He thinks, the common Reafon of Mankind
Will clear her of the fenfelefs Imputation.
But, what is Reafon, when ungodly Prelates
Hoodwink the Mind ; and make us Fond of Darknefs ?
                                             Mark ;

Mark; if I judge amiſs. — This Charge of Treaſon,
Founded on Sorcery, and idle Tales,
May coſt Dame *Eleanor* her deareſt Life;
And be the Prelude to her Husband's Downfall.

York. I like it not.

Warw. Nor I.———
In Miſchief's dark Deſigns, *Rome* is Infallible!

Saliſb. This unexpected Summons from the King,
To meet in Parliament, to Morrow, — bodes———
What, ſhall I ſay?——— Perhaps, I over-rate
The Policy of Knaves.——— And yet, I know,
The Proclamation was not *Glouceſter's* Doing.

Warw. But, — ſee where *Beaufort* comes:———
    The Cardinal,
Who bears his Head aloft, beneath his Hat,
And looks with Scorn on Princes.

York. Hence, my Lords!———
His conſecrated Pride offends my Eye.

Warw. To me, it miniſters but daily Mirth.

York. We leave you to your Humour.

Warw. But a Moment.

S C E N E II.

Warwick.   Beaufort.

Warw. How he collects his Brow!——— Intent on
    Miſchief:
His own ambitious Views; — or, *Glouceſter's* Ruin.

Beauf. Firſt, to diſgrace him, in his Wife:——— In
    That,
We gratify the Queen; who, now, expects us.

Warw. Save you, my good Lord Cardinal.———
    You ſeem
To ſtoop; as burden'd with ſome weighty Thought.

Beauf. Alas my Lord!——— It is my Grief ſits
    heavy.

Warw. Grief, for the Lady's Innocence; — I fear.
Beauf.

Beauf. So would my Nephew *Gloucefter* have reply'd. ——

But ; — of Her Innocence, the reverend Bifhops
Will give their upright Judgments. — Heaven knows,
My Heart is void of Malice, — as of Favour :
And, — were it not, my Brethren might fufpect
Me partial for the Honour of my Niece ;
I would, my felf, affift upon her Trial.

Warw. Come, come ; my Lord of *Winchefter* : —
For fhame,
Prevent a Complot of fo foul a Nature !
And free the Dutchefs ; — for the Kingdom's Quiet.

Beauf. Wherefore am I reproached ? —— Can I
reftrain,
Or, can I turn afide, the Courfe of Law ?

Warw. But if, in Times of zealous Ignorance,
A Law be made, which Reafon difannulls ; ——

Beauf. *Warwick*, — no more : — Thy Mind is li-
bertine. ——

If thou think'ft Witchcraft, but a fabled Crime ;
To Morrow, may'ft Thou, in free Parliament,
Declare in Favour of that deadly Sin,
Our holy Church condemns. — Mean time, We truft,
The Lord Protectour's Wife is innocent.

S C E N E III.

Warwick.

Farewell, Hypocrify and Pride ! —— Grey Hairs,
And griping Hands ! —— Ambitious ; — harfh, and
dreadfull,
Even to thy Friends ! —— What a Difgrace, that
Men, —
That Kings, fhould ftand in Awe of fuch a Pageant !
A Shew of Sanctity, trick'd up in Scarlet.
Believe in Sorcery ? —— No, Cardinal ! —
Thy Wit is not fo dull. —— What have the Laity

To

To do with Faculties, They dare not ufe? ——
Reafon, in Us, is Carnal. —— Beafts that we are ;
To fuffer *Rome* to fhackle our free Thoughts,
And fool our very Senfes! —— But, Soft. ——
Here comes the Sovereign Power! — Our female Ruler :
In Feature Woman ; but, in Heart, a Man :
Fair as the Queen of Beauty; Bold, as *Mars*. ——
And fee, how *Suffolk* gently moulds her Hand ;
And whifpers Things, — not fitting for My Ear.

S C E N E IV.

Queen Margaret.   *Duke of* Suffolk.   *Cardinal* Beaufort.

    Queen. Still in our Favour, *Suffolk* fhalt Thou Stand
The Foremoft. —— Well ; my Lord Cardinal : —
     How goes
The Bufinefs of the Day ? - - Is *Eleanor*
Adjudged ? — Or, muft her Treafon profper ;
And *Henry's* Life fubmit to magick Spells ?
That She may place the Crown on *Gloucefter's* Brow ;
And drive Us, like a Vagrant, from the Realm.
    Suff. Firft, perifh the Protectour, and his Friends!
    Beauf. Have better Hopes. —— Within Saint Ste-
     phen's Chappel,
This Hour, and more, the Spiritual Court is fate :
In which, prefides his Grace of *Canterbury*.
    Queen. I fear his Courage. —— Is he firm of Pur-
     pofe ?
Does he not dread that overbearing *Gloucefter ?*
Can he defpife the clamouring Populace ;
And prize the Friendfhip of a grateful Queen ?
    Beauf. Fear not for *Chicheley*, Madam : Moft Or-
     thodox,
In every Point ; the Scourge of Hereticks.
He will not be inclin'd to ftrain for Mercy
Toward One, turn'd Profelyte to *Wickliff's* Errours.
        B 3   *Queen.*

Queen. But, will your Evidence inforce Convicti-
on ? ———

For, oftentimes in Courts, when Doubts arife,
Do Crimes evade the Intention of the Law.

Suff. The Queen obferves judicioufly. ——— There
lies

The very Strefs of all our Hopes. ——— How fay you,
My Lord of *Winchefter?* ——— For fhould we fail
In this Attempt ; ———

Beauf. *Suffolk* ; — goe tutour Boys ! ———
I will not fail, — as Thou did'ft fail, in *France*. —
If you approve not of my Working ; — So ! ———
Get abler Heads.

Queen. The Duke is over-zealous. ———
We doubt not of your Policy ; long vers'd
In Court-Intrigues. ——— But, this Affair is Nice ;
And, as it turns, Duke *Humfrey* ftands, or falls.

Beauf. Let, who will, fall ; — Juftice muft hold
her Sway.

Such Witneffes are ready to confirm
Each Circumftance of the notorious Fact,
That this proud Dame fhall haunt the Court, no more ;
Nor yet, abide within the Church's Pale : ———
And then, — her Life will be at our Difpofal.

Suff. Yours be the Merit : ———
Queen. And accept My Thanks.

Oh, *Beaufort !* ——— Gratify my Soul in This ;
And Thou may'ft ask, ——— ask any Recompence ! ———
Thy Wealth, — vaft as it is, Thou fhalt account it
poor !

Drain from all Parts : — Accumulate, at Will !

Beauf. Alas, I covet not ! ——— Of honeft Gains
I would have Store, indeed ; — for pious Ufes.

Suff. Your Eminency is too Good, we know, —
Too Wife ; — to miffapply your Wealth. ——— But, fee :
The Duke of *Buckingham.*

S C E N E

SCENE V.

The Queen. *Duke of* Suffolk. *Cardinal* Beaufort. *Duke of* Buckingham.

Beauf. What of Dame *Eleanor?* —
Queen. Speak *Buckingham.* ——
Buckin. Madam, the Trial is over.
Queen. But, how? ——
Buckin. I heard her Doom pronounced. —
Queen. Give me the Words. ——
Pronounce it o'er again: — Miſs not a Tittle.
 Buckin. The Biſhops were unanimous: — When, from his Throne,
Old, venerable *Chicheley*, thus, gave Sentence
" Dame *Eleanor*; — Thou ſtand'ſt convict of Sor-
 " cery: —
" Sorcery moſt foul, againſt the Lord's Anoinced;
" Our Sovereign Liege: — A Crime, that merits
 " Death. —
" For which Offence, thy Penance is; Bare-foot,
" To paſs along, through the wide City Streets;
" Carrying a lighted Taper in thy Hand: —
" That every Witneſs of Thy publick Shame
" May ſee, No Dignity is rais'd above
" The Cenſure of the Church. ——
 Queen. Proceed. — What, more? —
Pauſe, yet, a While; and recollect the Whole.
 Buckin. " This done; — Cloſe Priſoner, in the Iſle
 " of *Man*,
" Remain in Penitence: — And ask, of Heaven, For-
 " giveneſs.
Such, Madam, is the Sentence on the Dutcheſs;
Who is conducted to the Palace Priſon.
 Beauf. A merciful Award, for ſuch a Crime!
 Queen. It is ſufficient, *Beaufort!* — Let her Live: —
Live Infamous; — far, from her Lord, divided; —
     The

The publick Scorn ;—— Derifion of the Court!

Beauf. I know, your Majefty does not require
Extremity of Juftice :——

   Queen. No!—— Let her live!—— To Age, in An-
      guifh pine :

And, late, enjoy the Happinefs of Death.

   Oh, my Lord Cardinal ; *Suffolk* ; *Buckingham !* ——
Condemn me not, my Friends, if I rejoice,——
If I exult, in *Eleanor's* Confufion!——
Have I not Reafon?—— Was I not her Queen ?——
Yet who, but She, of All the Nobles Wives,
O'erlook'd my Rank ; and vied with Me, in Gran-
     deur ?——
When She appear'd, loaded with Gold and Jewels,
Sweeping her Train along ; All Eyes She drew :
While I ftood, difregarded, in the Circle ;
Or pafs'd, unheeded, through the Throng of Courtiers.

   Now,——let her draw All Eyes :—— Now, let them
     gaze
Their Fill ;—— as, through the crouded Streets, She
   walks
In Penance :—— Till, wounded with Revilings,
Remorfe be fix'd, for ever, in her Soul!——
But,—— I have done.—— *Beaufort* ; Thy Thought is
   bufy.
Unfold thy Mind.

   Beauf. On this Succefs,—— methinks,——
Another might be rais'd ;—— of higher Import.——

   Queen. As how?

   Suff. Difclofe it to the Queen.

   Beauf. Somewhat,——
More tending—— to the Honour—— of the King.

   Queen. Speak out ; good Cardinal.

   Beauf. And yet,—— my Zeal,
Perhaps, is over-fedulous.

   Buckin. Fear not.——
Suffolk and I fhall not betray the Secret :——

   Suff. Nor, ftart from any Purpofe,—— here, approv'd.
                       Beauf.

Beauf. What, though the Duke of *Glouce*ster be a
  Man,
Not lightly moved?—— Yet,—— can I well conceive,
His doating Love for *Eleanor* will raife
A Ferment in his Blood.——— Confiding in his Power,
And, defperate to prevent her publick Shame;
He may be wrought to fuch a Pitch of Rafhnefs,
That We, at once, may lift him from his Office:——
His Ufurpation of the Sovereign Power.

  Queen. That were a Mafter-Stroke, in Policy!

  Beauf. Not, that I bear Difpleafure to my Ne-
    phew.———
But,—— while he ftiles himfelf the Lord Protectour;
He does eclipfe the Luftre of the Crown:——

  Suff. That, in Another, would be conftrued Trea-
    fon:——

  Buckin. Nor, is it lefs, in Him.

  Queen. What think you, then; my Lords?——
Seems not the Cardinal to counfell wifely?

  Suff. I think, the Event will anfwer to our Wifhes.

  Buckin. It cannot fail.

  Queen. Then,—— am I Queen, indeed!———

  Beauf. Or,—— fhould our Expectation fail.—— Why,
    then;——
We think,—— again,—— You, my Lord *Buckingham,*
Find *Glouce*ster out;—— and, fharpen his Refentments:
While I prepare my Brethren, to affert
The Juftice of their Sentence.

  Queen. May your Purpofe
Prove as fuccefsful, as the Hopes are pleafing

S C E N E VI.

The Queen. Duke of Suffolk.

  Queen. Protectour of the Realm!—— It muft not
    be.——

  Suff. And yet,—— how long, have We endur'd his
    Sway!
                                                    Queen.

Queen. Is not the King of Years to rule? —— Be-
    fide; —
It turns to My Dishonour: —— And, my Father,
In all his Letters, chides my mean Submission. ——
Must I be *Gloucester's* Pupil, too? —— Oh, *Suffolk!*
If Thou doeft love me; — If Thou lov'ft Thy felf;
As thou haft feated me on *England's* Throne,
Let me not be control'd; —— Affift, — refolve,
To refcue me from fuch Difgrace!

  Suff. By thofe bright Charms,
That heavenly Form, which captivates my Soul;
Your *Suffolk* will employ his utmoft Skill,
His whole Endeavours; rifque his Life and Fame,
To humble haughty *Gloucester* to your Nod! ——
And thofe fair Hands fhall hold the Reins of Empire.

  Queen. Then, fhall my *Suffolk* fhare the Rule with
    Me! —
A Rule, too turbulent for *Henry's* Meeknefs.

  Suff. But, — fhould Duke *Humfrey* fee the King; —

  Queen. I know —
His Prefence overaws him. —— Leave, to Me,
That Care.

  Suff. Mean time, will I advife with *Beaufort*;
Whofe working Brain is bent on *Gloucester's* Ruin:
Not, for Your Service, Madam; — nor, the King's; —
But, to deftroy the Man, who Twice accus'd him,
And Studies to defeat his whole Ambition.

  Queen. Fear not his towering Hopes. — When the
    Time comes,
We fhall exclude him from Saint *Peter's* Chair.

S C E N E

SCENE VII.

A Prison; belonging to the Palace.

Dutchess of Gloucester.

By false Accusers,— by invented Crimes,—
My Enemies have triumphed.—— Even their Mer-
    cy,—
May I not call it Cruelty?—— My Death
Had set a speedy Period to their Malice;—
And, placed my Soul above the Rage of *Rome.*
   O, Thou eternal Power, whose piercing Eye
Discerns each secret Guilt;— search thou my Heart!—
And, as Thou know'st Me innocent, support me;—
And, to the World, acquit my blemish'd Fame.
   But, here comes One, who doubles my Affliction.—

SCENE VIII.

Dutchess of Gloucester. *Duke of* Gloucester.

Dutch. O, *Gloucester!*— Lord of my Desires!—
    My Glory!—
Oh,— wherefore should'st Thou visit Thy Disho-
    nour?—
Fain would I hide my Shame from Thee!— Be gone;
And leave me to my Penance.
   Duke. No,— *Eleanor:*
Sooner, would I submit to the Indignity!
   Think'st thou, that *Gloucester's* Wife shall be ex-
    pos'd?—
A Spectacle to gaping Crouds;— the Mock
Of every vulgar Tongue!——
   Dutch. My dearest Lord;
For Your loved Sake, I wish, it might not be!

                      Duke.

Duke. For Thy lov'd Sake, it fhall not : — Come, —
   what may!

Audacious Prelates! — Minifters of *Rome!* —
Moft wicked Agents to the infernal Foe! —
Could I have fufpected you of fuch Prefumption,
You never fhould have judg'd Her Innocence. ——
But, I defy your infamous Tribunal!
Upheld by Frauds, and fuperftitious Fears. —
Are there not Crimes, fufficient, in the World ;
But You muft raife fantaftick Trefpaffes,
And tyrannize by Fables? —— Foul Delufions!

   Dutch. If, to be zealous in the Search of Truth ;
If, to abhorr foul Errours, be a Crime ;
Then, is my heavy Condemnation juft : ——
If Heaven thinks otherwife ; — Heaven be my Com-
   fort!

   Duke. Enough, my Love. —— For better Purpofes
Referve thy Tears. —— Thy Vertue is thy Guilt. —
But ; I will turn it to their own Confufion.

A waxen Image, — to deftroy the King! ——
No ; — bafe Impoftors! —— Your pernicious Counfels,
Rome's gainful Superftitions, are His Bane ;
The People's Grievance, and the King's Reproach.

Sweet *Eleanor,* — difmifs thy needlefs Grief. —
Thou fhalt not fuffer.

   Dutch. But, — the Church injoins it. ——
And, who fhall dare oppofe What They decree?

   Duke. Oppofe Iniquity? — Impiety? — and Craft? —
And Pride? — And Infolence ; beyond Support! ——
Are there no Free, — no Righteous, *Englifh* Spirits?
Has the Protectour, then, no Power? No Friends? ——
What? — Give thee up, — a Sacrifice to Falfehood!
And be the Scoff of *Beaufort* ; and of *Suffolk* ;
And, of that Queen ; — indigent *Reiner's* Daughter! —
Judge not, fo meanly, of thy *Gloucefter's* Love.

   Dutch. Alas, my Lord ; your Love and your high
   Courage
Make you o'erlook the Dangers, I forefee!

                                             The

The Punishing of Me is but a Snare
For *Gloucester's* Life.—— Should You, to rescue me,
Exert your Power, and summon all your Friends;
Your Enemies, combin'd, will call it Treason.

Duke. It is thy Tenderness creates these Fears!——
Fenced with Integrity, I live secure:
My Loyalty admits of no Suspicion.

Dutch. So, did you judge of Me.

Duke. Perfidious Wretches!——
They promis'd to acquit thee.—— But, no more.——
I will protect thee, still.—— The noblest Peers,
Whose Wives and Daughters are, in Thee, dishonour'd,
Are, All, concern'd; and will avenge this Outrage.
Ere now, thou had'st been set at Liberty;
But that, it seems, I am deny'd Admittance
To the King, my Nephew!—— That dowerless Queen
Has taken him to her Keeping.

Dutch. Be assur'd,
Beaufort and She, Both in Contrivance subtle,
Have plotted, deep, against your envied Power:——
And,— That destroy'd;—— Who answers for your Life?——
Oh, did you know the Terrours of my Heart,
You would not tempt the Malice of your Foes!

Duke. I tempt it not.—— But, I am stung,— to Death!——
And, how shall I divest my self of Feeling?——
Say, injur'd Innocence!—— What can I, more?

Dutch. Let your Resentment sleep.—— The patient Mind,
By yielding, overcomes.—— This shamefull Penance
Will turn, hereafter, to our lasting Praise;
When Men shall speak of *Eleanor's* Submission,
And *Gloucester's* brave Forbearance!—— Both, alike,
Preferring *England's* Quiet, to their Own.

Duke.

Duke. Excellent Woman!—— How doeſt Thou
  perſwade!

Dutch. This is no Time for Rage;— nor private
  Grudgings.——
The People's Diſcontents, the King's Affairs,
The Nation's Weal, require your cool Advice.

Duke. O, *Eleanor!*— In Vertue finiſh'd;——
  Wiſe,
Beyond thy Sex!— Well doeſt Thou caution me.

Dutch. Let them enjoy their poor Revenge, a
  While.——
Conſcious of no Offence,— Why ſhould I grieve?
Where Guilt is abſent, there can be no Shame.

Duke. But,— if I live,— I will repay their Malice.——

Fellow;— What would'ſt thou?—   {*Enter an Officer.*

Dutch. Good my Lord;— ſpeak gently.——
He comes to lead me forth, to——

Duke. Hence,— Miſcreant!

Dutch. I do beſeech you!—— Uſe your Modera-
  tion.

Duke. Begone!—— The Duke of *Gloucester* warns
  thee hence:——
The Lord Protectour warns thee;— on thy Life!

Dutch. Stay, Officer:— I come.—— The Duke
  forgets——
Sweet Heaven, appeaſe him, now!—— My Lord,——

Duke. I ſay,
Thou ſhalt not goe;— till I appoint the Time.——
Nay;— Never, will I ſuffer thee to goe!——
Nor, ſhalt thou, Here, abide.—— I am determin'd!——
If, it be Raſhneſs;—— Let me, then, be raſh;——
Let me be deſperate!— in thy Defence.——
The People,— All, will juſtify my Conduct.

Dutch. O, my lov'd *Gloucester!*— Oh, recall! your
  Reaſon.——

                                                We

We ftand upon a Precipice! —— Thus, kneeling,
Do I fupplicate. —— Preferve your felf; —— and
    Me: —
Preferve the King; — Preferve the publick Peace :—
And, make not Me the Caufe of civil Difcord.
    Duke. Rife, then, — Thou gentle Calmer of my
      Breaft ;
Balm of my wounded Soul! —— I am refign'd. ——
I will incur no Blame. —— Goe, then! —— But; —
    when
This Penance is perform'd; —— Thou muft away! ——
    Yet, — fhall the Sea, not long, divide our Loves.
Thou fhalt return :—— Or, I will haften after.
    Dutch. Mean Time, —— Adieu. —— Each
    Night, —
Each lonely Hour, — will I not ceafe to pray
For *England*'s Happinefs and *Gloucefter*'s Safety.
    Duke. Heaven have thee in Protection! —— This
      Embrace, —
    Dutch. And — This; —— my Lord! ——
    Duke. Oh, — *Eleanor* ! ——
    Dutch. Nay, — do not grieve. ——
    Duke. Do Thou
Not grieve. ——
    Dutch. Once more, — — Adieu.
    Duke. Oh, — ftay! —— And, take —
The tendereft Rapture of my Soul, — to cherifh! ——

S C E N E IX.

Duke of Gloucefter.

Then, — by my Sufferings, *Beaufort* ! —— And
    Thou, *Suffolk* ! —
And *Margaret*, —— Difhonour of the King! ——
Howe'er I bear it outwardly ; — think not,
That *Gloucefter* lives, Infenfible of Wrongs! ——
                       And

And, you have Wrong'd me, — Where I feel it
    Moſt!
    But ; — let it ſleep.——— The publick Wrongs
    redreſs ;
And, thy own painfull Griefs, a While, ſuppreſs.
Within thy Breaſt, compoſe the doubtfull Strife :
Thy Countrey, firſt, relieve ; and then, — thine in-
    jur'd Wife.

End of the Firſt A C T.

ACT II. SCENE I.

Beaufort.   *Suffolk.*

Beaufort.

INdeed, my Lord, it is a Difappointment.——
  I did not think, my Nephew *Gloucefter* could
    have been
So Meek!—— Perhaps,— his Love is in the Wane.
  Suff. Rather fufpect, He Stifles his Refentment;
Deferring Vengeance, to make Vengeance Sure.
  Beauf. It is not in his Nature.— A froward In-
    fant,
As foon, may be inftructed to diffemble.
And yet,— He thinks himfelf exceeding Wife!
And, the poor Commons praife him, for a Statefman.
  Suff. I know not, What to hope; nor, What to
    fear.—
But, I repent, we did, fo rafhly, fhew
Our Enmity:— A fruitlefs Provocation;
Since, it impairs not his eftablifh'd Power.
  Beauf. Why This to Me?—— Can I befpeak
    Events?——
It was the Queen's Defire:— You know, it was.
  Suff. You turn too quick upon my Thought!—
    I grant,
It was the Queen's Defire.— But, moftly She de-
    mands,
That the Protectour's Power be overthrown.

C

Beauf.

Beauf. Not, in an Inftant ; fure!— My good
  Lord *Suffolk.*—·

A little Patience ;— and it may be done.

Suff. But ; let us ftill be mindful,— that, to Morrow,—

Beauf. Firft, let to Morrow come!— Or,— come
  This Night!—

In That fhort Interval, may lie, conceal'd,

An Hour, that fhall determine *Humfrey*'s Rule.

Suff. I grow impatient!—— That, the Glaſs of
  Time

Had, Now, begun to meaſure out That Hour!

Beauf. Suppoſe him, then exaſperated:— Whether,

For *Eleanor*'s Diſgrace ;— Or, being refus'd

To ſ e the King:— Or, Both.— Ere Night, he may,

With Indignation ftung, give up his Office.——

Not, that I build Thereon.— He may, to Morrow,

Be abſent from a Parliament, thus ſummon'd,

Without confulting Him. Or,— at the Worft ;—

Let us ſuppoſe,— he ſhou'd appear,— prepar'd ;—

With all his Friends, to Noiſe it on his Side!——

Suff. Ay, my Lord Cardinal:— That Suppoſi-
  tion!—

Beauf. Yet,— even then, we undertake to triumph!

Suff: Therein, I do confeſs, My Foreſight fails.

Confider,— He is eloquent of Speech ;

In Utterance, bold : And, has obtain'd ſuch Credit,

That All aſſent to What His Lips averr.

Then,— there is *Warwick* ; of a Wit, engageing ;

Keen, in Debate ; and ready, to reply :

And,— *York* ; who pours a Torrent of Diſcourſe :

And,— *Salisbury* ; of a dangerous Diſcernment.

How can We ftem this Tide of Enmity ?

Beauf. By ſuperiour Skill.— Since, we are em-
  bark'd,

We muft not faint : But, fteady, fteer our Courfe.

                                                    Two

Two Tempests, rais'd by *Gloucester* and his Faction,
Allready have I weather'd! ——
Suff. My Doubts arise,
Not out of Fear; but, Caution. — Propose
Some Speedy Counsel, for our common Safety.
Beauf. First, — let his Majesty prepare a Speech ; —
A Speech, wherein He thanks the Duke, his Uncle,
For his long, faithful Services: — Then, adds;
That, Now, in Manhood ripe, his Sovereign Dignity
Demands, the Lord Protectour's Office should expire.
Suff. This will not be displeasing to the King.
Beauf. Or, if it should; — the Queen must, then,
    employ
Her powerful Influence. — That Point secur'd ;
We must be diligent : Try every Art
To canvass Voices : — Win over some, with Hopes ;
And some, with Fears , — And, buy our spendthrift
    Lords,
And needy Commons.
Suff. It seems a happy Thought !
But here comes *Gloucester :* — And, — in his Coun-
    tenance,
Displeasure lowrs.
Beauf. As I could wish ! —— Let us
Abide his Frowns ; —— and, found his Discontents.

S C E N E II.

Beaufort. Suffolk. Gloucester.

Glouceſt. Say, Duke of *Suffolk* ; and You, my reve-
    rend Uncle ;
What is my Crime ; — that I am, thus, deny'd
Admittance to the King? —— I thought, my Office,
My Right of Blood, and my unwearied Services,
Might, every Hour, intitle me to a Hearing :
Whether to advise ; request ; or, to remonstrate.
Suff. Suffolk does not presume to blame the King ;

Nor

Nor yet, to charge your Highneſs with a Crime.

Beauf. Perhaps,—— his Majeſty is indiſpos'd :
Perhaps,—— it is His Pleaſure to be private.
What have the Duke, and I, to do?—— The King
Is of full Years to regulate his Conduct ;
And, may conſult, When, and with Whom, He pleaſes.

   Glouceſt. I underſtand you Both.—— Let the King's
   Conduct,
Let all his Actions (copying his great Father!)
Tend to the Advancement of his own Renown ;
The Nation's Honour ; and the People's Welfare :
And, *Glouceſter* is indifferent, Who adviſes ;
Or, Whence proceed ſuch glorious Reſolutions.

   Beauf. For thoſe great Ends (no doubt) our Royal
   Nephew
Means to conſult the Council of the Nation :——
And, Heaven direct them !

   Suff. You, my Lord Protector,
Suſpending, for a Time, domeſtick Cares,
Will not be abſent from our Conſultations.——
Account it ſome Relief, that, for Your Sake,
All good Men grieve, the Dutcheſs ſhould incurr
Such heavy Cenſure.

   Glouceſt. I diſdain the Inſult!
This poor Diſſimulation!— 'Tis ignoble.——
I, ne'er, could learn ſuch Meanneſs toward my Foes!

   To You, my Lord,— and to That Cardinal,—
And — to the Queen, I ſtand indebted, for
The rude Treatment of my Wife.—

   Beauf. She deſerv'd it.

   Glouceſt. That is a Slander, ill-becomes thy Prieſt-
   hood !——

   Beauf. Was ſhe not ſentenced by due Courſe of
   Law?
Though, ſentenced ſhort,— far ſhort, of Her De-
merits!

   Glouceſt. Her whole Demerits are, That, in Religion,

She

She reafons more, perhaps, than You allow :
Perhaps rejects, as frivolous and vain,
What Churchmen teach of Witchcraft, and of Spells.
She, likewife, may have given fome flight Offence
To our fair Niece ;—— this Queen ! — of *Suffolk's*
   making.
  To thefe Demerits add, that *Gloucefter* loves her ;
That She is Wife to the Protectour. ———— Thefe,
And Thefe, alone, are *Eleanor's* Demerits !
  Beauf. She cleaves to *Wickliff's* Herefie !—— De-
  clare
That boafted Merit to the Spiritual Court ;
And, give her up to Flames :—— And, clear thy
  felf
Of all Sufpicion. ————
  Glouceft. Moft degenerate *Beaufort !*
Thou bafe-born Offspring of brave *Lancafter* ;
My famous Grandfire :—— Doeft thou, then, dif-
  turb
Thy bleffed Father's Reft ?—— The mighty Patron
Of learned *Wickliff*, and His Followers.
  Beauf. Dares,
Then, the Protectour of the Realm avow ——
  Suff. Lord Cardinal ; no farther urge his Highnefs :
Since, as a Husband, he is much incens'd.
  Beauf. Not fo, my Lord. —— His Hatred to the
  Church
He fhews ;— more, than his conjugal Affection.
  Glouceft. Audacious Prieft ! — Unworthy of the
  Garb
Of holy Men : Unhallowed, by thy Life ;
The Scandal of the Church ; — a Viper, in the
  State ! —
Thou Reprobate ! — Doeft Thou prefume to cenfure ?
  Malice, Hypocrify, Avarice, and Pride,
And Turbulency, and Ambition, — and
Lewd Defires (the Infamy of Age !)
Pollute thy facred Dignity ; and, ftain thy Robes :——

           Thofe

Thofe Robes (Thou know'ft) my Brother (well
    difcerning
Thy Sawcy Arrogance) did often charge thee,
On thy Allegiance, never to aflume.
　　Beauf. Then, *Gloucefter,* — by That facred Digni-
ty, henceforward
I fet thee at Defiance !—— And, in Return
To thy reproachfull Speech ; Thou art — a Traitour !
Thou doeft abett the Treafon of thy Wife ;
That darling Sorcerefs ! — Both trafficking with Hell,
To wafte the King, and to ufurp his Crown.
　　Glouceft. Wert thou the Sovereign Pontiff, triply
    crown'd,
That Calumny is the Forfeit of thy Life !——
Suffolk ; let goe ;——
　　Suff. I muft arreft your Fury.——
Let his Age, his holy Function, ftay your Arm.
　　Beauf. No, *Suffolk :*—— Let him execute his Pur-
pofe.
Let him imbrue his Hands in the innocent Blood
Of his old, feeble, and defencelefs, Uncle.
　　Glouceft. Curfe on the Kindred !—— Be doubly
    curs'd the Law,
Whereby thy cafual Birth became Legitimate :
Elfe, had'ft thou liv'd Obfcure ;— and, much lefs
    Guilty.
　　Beauf. I know my Crime ; the Source of all thy
    Rage.
I muft not live to curb thy headftrong Power ;
That Thou may'ft lord it, free from all Controll.
　　Glouceft. Live, fcorn'd !—— Live to make Good
    thy Charge of Treafon.
　　Full Five and Twenty Years, in Loyalty
Approv'd ; My Counfels, however crofs'd by Thee,
Did always tend to aggrandize my Nephew ;
The precious Pledge of his immortal Father !
　　When, yet, our Sovereign's Voice was infant Cries ;
A Cradle, for his Throne ;— Did, ever, I
　　　　　　　　　　　　　　　　　　(Taking

(Taking the Advantage of his tender Years)
Employ my Power, or practice on his Life,
To ftep into his Seat? —— Even, to this Hour,
Has the Protectour labour'd, to compofe
Our home-bred Factions, and unite the Nobles
In dutifull Subjection to their King.
   What Enmities, what Friendfhips have I made,
Through my Adminiftration; but, with Men,
Who are his beft of Friends, or worft of Foes?
   Perverfe old Man! Shamelefs Abufer! —— Know;
If, *Gloucefter* were difloyal; — if, I could
Betray my Truft, and ftoop to Ufurpation:
I fhould not have Recourfe to idle Spells;
But, to my Sword: — That Sword, which (with
   Succefs)
Under my godlike Brother's dreadfull Banner,
Has fought for *England*'s Glory; now declining,
Through *Beaufort*'s, and through *Suffolk*'s, wicked
   Counfels.
   Suff. To Morrow, *Gloucefter*, fpeak ——
   Beauf. Make no Reply.——
Your Grace perceives, He is not in a Temper
To reafon with his Friends. — He muft have time
To cool. ——

S C E N E III.

Gloucefter.

   Away! —— I would not learn from Thee! ——
Thou temperate Villain; in Unforgivenefs cool:
Who putteft a Glofs of Sanctity on Malice;
And feem'ft to weep, and feem'ft to pray, for thofe,
Thou would'ft deftroy. ——

C 4   S C E N E

S C E N E IV.

Gloucefter. Warwick. York.

Glouceft. Why droops the noble *York*, ———
And *Warwick* ; — ever wont to cheer his Friends ? —
Or, does the Difcompofure in My Looks,
Where Signs of inward Grief and Indignation
Appear confus'd, transform you to My Likenefs ?

York. What generous Breaft, but faddens, with your
    Highnefs !

Warw. What pitying Eye, feeing what We beheld,
But wept ; — as *Gloucefter*'s crimelefs Confort pafs'd,
In Penance rude, along the flinty Streets ! ———

York. And ever, when fome rugged Pebble wounds
Her tender-feeling Feet, the abject Rabble
Scoff, as fhe ftarts with Anguifh of the Pain ;
And, bid her be advifed, how fhe treads ; ———

Warw. While pale, and red, by Turns, with guilt-
lefs Shame,
To Earth fhe bends, — fometimes to Heaven fhe lifts,
Her ruefull Eyes, — profufe of gufhing Tears. ———

Glouceft. No more ; my Friends. ——— Diftraction
    to my Soul ! ———
I apprehend you, well : And, you have rouz'd
My couching Rage. ——— Reproach me, then : And fay ;
Yet, *Gloucefter* lives ? — Yet, *Gloucefter* is a Prince ! —
Yet, *Gloucefter* is Protectour ! ——— But, I do renounce
My ignominious Patience : ——— Yes ; I will retrieve
My paft Neglect ; and vindicate my Love.

Warw But ; — She is gone : A mournfull, widow'd Exile !

Glouceft. They fhall recall her : — E're I fleep, dif-
patch
Their Orders. ——— I will go my felf ; will bring
Her back, in Triumph ! — Will demand fuch Vengeance,

                                    That

That *Beaufort*, and the *Queen*, fhall rue my Wrath:
Shall curfe their Malice; their Succefs: And feel,
That injur'd Patience, kindled into Rage,
Is fierce;—— is fatal, as the long-pent Thunder,
That fhoots the deftin'd Bolt with double Fury!

 York. Let *Gloucefter* but refolve; We come, determin'd,
To ftand the foremoft Champions in your Caufe.

 Warw. It is the King's,—— it is the Nation's,
  Caufe!
Both abus'd, by a reftlefs, bafe-defigning, Fac-
  tion. ——
O, call to Mind, the mighty Hoft of Friends,
Who Wait but Your Command. ————

 Glouceft. There lies my Dread! ———— And, I
  retract my Rage.
The King's, the Nation's, Caufe is, Now, at Ven-
  ture:
And, Heaven forbid, My Wrongs, however grievous,
Should ftir the People up to rude Commotions.

 Rather, let *Gloucefter's* Friends, and chiefly You,
And *Salisbury* (for his Wifdome juftly famed)
Affift, to ftill the Murmurs of the People;
And reconcile the Commons to the King.

 Warw. We, and our Followers, are prepar'd to forward
Thofe Meafures, the Protectour fhall approve.

 York. Muft, then, your Vertue fuffer? ——

 Glouceft. Oh, my Friends!——
Let not My Sufferings interfere with Aught,
That may concern the Happinefs of Thoufands.

 Why, was I born a Prince?— Why, fingled out
To ward the King?— The Pilot of the State,
Juft foundering in continual Storms of Faction!

 Had Providence difpos'd my Lot, more humble;
Not placed me high, within the publick View;
But, led me in the private Paths of Life:
Then,— *Eleanor,*— Thy Happinefs, Thy Wrongs,
             Thine

Thine every Wifh, had been my chief Regard!
　Excufe, my Lords, this Weaknefs, in your Friend. ——
My ruffled Thoughts are, yet, unapt for Bufinefs.
This Evening (when I fhall be more compos'd)
Expect me, to confult againft to Morrow.
　York. Your Highnefs will appoint the Hour.
　Gloucest. At Eight.
　York. The Place.
　Gloucest. At *Warwick*'s.
　Warw. Thither, will I affemble
A Band of Patriots; — Men, approv'd by *Gloucester*.

S C E N E V.

York. Warwick.

　York. Thou Father to the King; and, to thy Coun-
　　trey!
How ill are all thy Services requited?
　Warw. Well, do the People ftile Thee Good; Thou,
　　Beft
Of Men! —— But, what avails thy Goodnefs? While
Henry is befet with Priefts and Sycophants;
And that imperious *Margaret* wrefts the Scepter,
From his weak Hand, employ'd to finger Beads.
　York. Slaves that we were! —— Did *Suffolk* merit
　　Thanks,
For treating this unreputable Match;
By *Gloucester*, difapprov'd?
　Warw. Thofe hafty Thanks
We may recall. —— But, fee; — my Father feeks
　　us.

S C E N E

SCENE VI.

York. Warwick. Salisbury.

Salisb. What think you, Now ? —— Were Mine,
    but vain Surmises ?
Or, was the Net spred, only, for the Dutchess ?
    York. What farther Mischiefs, *Salisbury*, do you trace ?
    Salisb The Duke, and all His Friends (expressly
    We)
Are shut out from the King, now sate in Council. ——
And yet, the Parliament is held, to Morrow !
    By this Procedure, it seems evident,
They mean to set aside the Lord Protectour.
    Warw. Then, *England*, bid Adieu to all thy Hopes !
    York. Before they can divest him of his Office,
They must obtain the Parliament's Concurrence.
    Salisb. Even That may be obtain'd. —— But,
    Where is *Gloucester* ?
Or, lives he, still, supine ; wrapt up, in his
Integrity ?
    Warw. This Evening, at My House,
We are to meet him.
    York. But, with his wonted Goodness,
He gives up his Resentments to the State ;
And does intreat, His Wrongs may not be mention'd.
    Warw. Even the fond Husband to the Patriot yields !
    Salisb. That honest Men should be so blinded by
Their Vertue ! — So devoid of Jealousy !
    York. My Heart is troubled for the banish'd Dutchess.
    Salisb. Know, then ; I have prevail'd with Sir *John*
    Stanley,
To keep his Prisoner here, a Day, at least. ——
But, of This, the Duke is not to be inform'd.
Let Him believe her, gone ; ——
    Warw. Or, He would visit her,
This Night. ——

                                                    York,

York. That muft not be.——
Salisb. But, to return.———
Malice towards Him, is Malice towards the Pub-
    lick ! —

How fhall we fave the State, if He be ruin'd ?
And, how prevent His Ruin, if we fuffer
Thefe wicked Counfellours, about the King ?
    York. And, how remove them from his Perfon ?
    Salisb. By Attainder.——
Their Crimes will furnifh out a Charge, to crufh
The Mignion of the Queen, her new-made Duke,
And that old Serpent, *Beaufort*.
    Warw. Thefe remov'd ;
Deluded *Buckingham* has no Support.
    Salisb. Let other Bufinefs wait, 'till This be done.
    What, though the mean Artificers did make
A Holiday ? — What, though the houfelefs Crew,
Who live upon the Dole of Priefts, did fhout ?——
The Citizens, the Commoners, the Peers,
All, who have Senfe of Vertue, mourn'd to fee
Good *Gloucefter*'s Wife abus'd. All cry aloud,
We will avenge the good Duke *Humfrey!*—— This
    Occafion,
The laft we e'er may have, muft not be loft.
    York. 'Tis well advis'd, my Lord : You lay, before
    us,
The Danger, and the Safety, of the Nation.——
We muft begin by weeding out thefe Traitours.
    What profits all the Plowman's Skill and Pain,
If Tares and Brambles choke the rifing Grain ?
What Force have Laws to make the People bleft,
If factious Spirits do the State moleft ?

End of the Second A C T.

ACT III.   SCENE I.

Beaufort.   Buckingham.

Beaufort.

YOU may rely upon my Information.——
    I paid a liberal Price, to learn the Secret.
  Buck. Then, my Lord Cardinal, we ftand in Need
Of all your Forecaft. — It asks, both Force and Skill,
To ward the heavy Stroke of an Attainder.
  Beauf. Be not difmay'd.— Fear nurfes up a Dan-
    ger:
And Refolution kills it, in the Birth.
  The Dye is caft!
  Buck. You fhall approve Me, ftedfaft.
  Beauf. Our Time is fhort:— The Night draws
    on, apace.——
The Queen, and *Suffolk*, muft be found. — In Him,
Our Safety lies.— 'Tis well, our Foes attempt
His Life, with Mine.———
  Buck. Behold them Both.
  Beauf. Mark, then,
How we fhall Work upon Her tender Fears.

SCENE

S C E N E. II.

Beaufort. Buckingham. Queen. Suffolk.

Queen.   At laft, my Lord of *Winchefter,* the King
Will nor have *Gloucefter,* longer, bear the Title,
Nor derogating Office, of Protectour :
And, if a Woman be allow'd to judge,
The Speech is well-adapted to our Purpofe.
　　Beauf.   But, Madam; That is not Sufficient, Now.
　　Suff.   Yet, is it not a Matter to be flighted.
　　Beauf.   I flight it not.———— But, *Suffolk,* we muft
　　　take,
Yet bolder Meafures; and, with Speed: Or, all
Our paft Endeavours ————
　　Queen.   What new Obftacles ?
　　Beauf.   Our Enemies are alarm'd for the Protec-
　　　tour.————
This Night, do *Gloucefter, Salisbury, Warwick, York,*
(With many more of their Cabal) affemble,
At *Warwick's,* to contrive ————
　　Queen.   What can they, There,
Contrive ?— The King is Ours.
　　Buckin.   What Favourites dread :—
The never-failing Means to curb their Power.
　　Suff.   What Mifchief ?
　　Beauf.   An Attainder.
　　Queen.   Againft Whom ?————
What Favourites dread !— Speak, *Buckingham ;* Speak,
　　Beaufort :
Who are to fall the Victims to their Rage ?
　　Beauf.   My Self ;— and *Suffolk.*
　　Queen.   *Suffolk !*— did'ft thou fay ?
　　Beauf.   It may be,— *Buckingham* will not cfcape.
　　Queen.   But, anfwer as to *Suffolk !*
　　Beauf.   Chiefly Him !

　　　　　　　　　　　　　　　　Queen.

Queen. Pernicious Prelate!— Medling, hoary Trai-
tour!
Attempting all Things; and, performing Nothing!
Is This the Fruit of thy malicious Counfels?——
Were we not prompted on, by Thee?— Did'ft Thou
Not forge the Crime? Did'ft Thou not, bafely, hire
Falfe, perjur'd Witnefles? —— The King fhall know it:
Gloucefter fhall be Protectour, ftill: The Dutchefs
Shall have ample Recompence,— from Thee;
And double all her Sufferings, on Thy Head!——
  Suff. Let me intreat your Majefty ——
  Queen. No, *Suffolk!*——
I fee my Errour;— Thy Ruin, and my Own!—
I know the formidable Power, againft us:
I know, My Marriage, and the giving up
Of *Maine* and *Anjou,* will be urg'd, to Morrow,
To Thy Deftruction.—— We muft join with *Glou-
cefter;*
Ask his Forgivenefs:— And, renounce this Cardinal;
This wily,— this moft inaufpicious, Prieft.——
But; 'Tis the Curfe of bufy, ambitious Churchmen,
Ever to plot; and, Never, to fucceed!
  Beauf. Now, give an injur'd Prelate leave to Speak;
But, not in Words of Bitternefs.— Your Majefty,
And *Suffolk,* may renounce me:— Yet, is *Beaufort*
Not deftitute of Friends.—— The Mitred Powers,
Bifhops and Abbots, and the Holy See,
Protect My Innocency.— Let Others feek
For Shelter, where they may!——
  Suff. Lord Cardinal,
Too haftily you take Offence.— Blame not
The Queen's Surprize.
  Beauf. I fhall not intermeddle:—
Nor, will I, vainly, fue for *Humfrey's* Favour.
The Queen (who knows him, better than his Uncle)
May find Acceptance, for her try'd Affection
To *Eleanor:*——
  Queen. Moft infolent Seducer!——

Beauf.

Beauf. And *Suffolk*'s Services are fo notorious,
He cannot fear Injuftice from the Parliament.

Suff. My Lord of *Winchefter*; you know, the People,
Incens'd by our Proceedings, ———

Queen. Fear not, *Suffolk*!
This moody Parliament fhall be prorogued;
Month, after Month. — Or, if They, never, meet:
It is a Form, the King may, well, difpenfe with.

Suff. That, were to ruin Him; your Self; and,
Me.

Buck. Alas, your Majefty is, yet, a Stranger
To the free, ftubborn, Spirits of the *Englifh*! ———
Tenacious of their ancient Rights and Cuftoms,
They will not be controll'd, but by their Laws:
Nor, is the King, without his Parliament, fecure.

Queen. What can be done! —

Suff. Your Eminency fees,
The Queen would be advis'd.

Beauf. Not I. — Let Thofe
Advife, who covet an unthankfull Office.
Let them attaint: — We fhall appeal to *Rome*.

Queen. *Beaufort*, excufe a Woman's weak Alarms.
It is Affection, What you conftrue Rage:
It is a Dread, a Terrour, for my Friends!
Fain, would I turn afide the impending Mifchief;
And, want not Refolution, to attempt:
But, let me know, What is to be attempted!
Say then, my Lord; advife us, yet, once more;
And finifh That, you have fo well begun.

Beauf. There is but one Expedient, now to ex-
tricate
The King from Tutelage, and fave your Friends:
And You, alone, are equal to the Task.

Queen. Then, count it done, my Lords! — And,
count my Will,
In all Attempts, fuperiour to my Power.

Beauf. Thus, then: — The King muft be prevail'd upon

To

To grant an Order for the immediate Seisure
Of *Gloucester* ;— And his Servants.——

Suff. The Protectour!——

Beauf. Is *Suffolk* startled, then ? ——

Queen. *Beaufort,* proceed.

Beauf. I stand reprov'd.

Queen. An Order, you were saying,
To Seise the Lord Protectour, and his Servants :——
I like it well.

Beauf. Only upon Suspicion
(I mean) of Treason, to confine my Nephew
To his Apartment ;— For a Day, at most.

Queen. His Exclusion from the King will Countenance
This Order :——

Beauf. And, his Party, seeing that Stroke
Pursued, will be Confounded with Surmises.
Beside ;— It does prevent their Meeting Him,
At *Warwick's* :— And, we gain a Day, to vote
His Office, void.—— That Difficulty, conquer'd ;
The Parliament may be dissolv'd, at Pleasure.

Queen. *Suffolk,* and *Buckingham* ;— How say you,
Now ;

Suff. The Advice is bold : And, it may prove
successfull.

Buckin. It tallies, well, with what is done already.

Queen. I answer for the King :——

Beauf. And I, for *Gloucester* ;
That We shall never dread his Anger, more.

Queen. My Lord of *Winchester* ; You must with
Me.——
The King shall thank you.

Beauf. I decline, in Years.
When I am dead ; your Majesties will lose
An humble, faithful, unambitious, Servant.

SCENE III.

Buckingham. Suffolk.

Suff. Who is there, *Beaufort*, does not know Thee,
better!

Buckin. His Actions and his whole Deportment
glare,
Confpicuous, through the flender Veil of Words.

Suff. Such grofs Diffimulation (like a Mift,
Before fome Meteor) magnifies his Vices.

But, *Buckingham*, his Infolence muft pafs
Uncheck'd; 'till He has wrought his Spite on *Glou-
cefter:*
Then, caft him off!

Buckin. Herein, I dare believe
His Heart Sincere.

Suff. There is no Room for Doubt:
Since, *Gloucefter* is a Bar to his Ambition.

Yet, when the Lord Protectour is remov'd;
The Queen (who knows his prieftly Pride) refolves
To difappoint him of the Popedome. ——
Thus much, for Your Inftruction. —— Let him work
For Us. —— Let him fucceed; or, fail: —— In This,
His Malice is his only Recompenfe;
In That, we turn the Blame on Him, alone.

Buckin. He has difpers'd large Summs, to purchafe
Voices.

Suff. Urge him to More. —— His Treafures are
immenfe! ——
Nor, muft We fpare, on this Occafion.

Buckin. See! ——
The Lord Protectour.

Suff. We may learn his Bufinefs.

SCENE

S C E N E IV.

Buckingham. Suffolk. Gloucester.

Glouceſt. Since the King's Pleaſure is (if ſo it be)
That I remain excluded from his Councils;
I hope, I may, through *Suffolk*'s Interceſſion,
Speak to the Queen.
 Suff. The Queen! — My Lord Protectour ?
 Glouceſt. Why not, the Queen ?
I have no favour'd Whiſpers to impart.
You and the Duke your Friend, may hear my Buſineſs:
So, might the King.—— Nay more ; I give my Word,
You will be pleas'd with what I have to ſay.
 Suff. We aſk not What. ——Lord *Buckingham,* do
  You
Let the Queen know the Pleaſure of his Highneſs.
 Glouceſt. No! — Not my Pleaſure: —— But, my
  poor Requeſt.

S C E N E V.

Suffolk. Gloucester.

 Suff. Your Pardon, Sir: —— I did not mean Of-
  fence.
 Glouceſt. Vain-glorious *Suffolk* ; Yes! —— Through-
  out the long
Continuance of my high Power, I never us'd
Such Arrogance of Speech to my Inferiours :
And, Equals (Since my Brother *Bedford*'s Death)
Amongſt my Fellow-Subjects, have I None !
Nor, can I have ; untill a Prince of *Wales*
Be born.—— Nay ; frown not, Duke of *Suffolk!* ——
Duke, By your Treachery to the King, and to His
  Realm.

           Suff.

Suff. Our Frowns, perhaps, bear equal Dread with
    Yours.
The fame confenting Powers, that gave to you
Authority to be our Lord Protectour,
Have thought, My Services deferv'd their Thanks.
The Peace and Marriage have not been difpleafing
To the King and Parliament; however *Gloucefter*
May be offended.
    Glouceft. I do remember, well,
Thy boaftful Speeches; — How, thou did'ft beguile
The Lords and Commons of their publick Thanks. ——
But, Parliaments have, often, been furpris'd;
And, often, have retriev'd their paft Miftakes.
    Suffolk. Your arbitrary Sway demands their Notice.

S C E N E VI.

Suffolk. Gloucefter. Beaufort.

    Glouceft. Infult me not, proud Mignion! —— Thou
    art not
Privileged in abufive Words, like *Beaufort.*
    Beauf. Why, my Lord *Suffolk,* fhould you hold Dif-
    courfe
With over-boiling Choler? —— 'Tis his Temper:
It, ever, was. —— He thinks it, Manlinefs;
A moft Exalted Vertue! ——
    Glouceft. 'Tis a Temper,
An Opennefs of Heart, in which I glory;
The Failing (if you pleafe) of honeft Minds:
A Quality, unfafe for Men, like Thee!
    Beauf. A Quality, indeed, I envy not;
Content with Talents of an humbler Kind.
    Suff. The Queen. ——
We leave your Highnefs.
    Glouceft. I befeech you, ftay.
I will not, long, detain you: And, my Bufinefs
Regards the Publick; not, my own Concerns.

                    S C E N E

SCENE VII.

Suffolk.　Gloucester.　Beaufort.　Queen.

Queen. What would the Lord Protectour, then,
　with Us?

Glouceſt. That Title, Madam, is become a Crime;
The only Crime, that *Gloucefter* knows: Unlefs,
Your Majefty is pleas'd to inform me; Why,
A Prince, and Peer, of *England* is deny'd
Admittance to the King.

Queen. We come not, hither,
To anſwer Queſtions. —— I was told, you had
Some Bufinefs to impart. — If ſo; be brief.

Glouceſt. Madam, I know, Affairs of State demand
　you.
Brief, then: I would refign my needlefs Office;
Whether to you, or to the King.

Queen. I undertake,
My royal Confort will not be difpleas'd.

Glouceſt. He has no Will, but Yours. —— Before,
　you came
To grace the Court, My Counfels bore ſome Weight;
But, Your Superiour Wifdom makes them ufelefs:
And, I have held my Office, much too long.
Therein I merit Blame.

Queen. Yes; Scornful Man!
Too long thou haft held it; and, too proudly,
　govern'd:
As if, while *Gloucefter* lives, the Majefty
Of *England* muft fubmit to Tutelage;
And, be the Scorn of all the Neighbouring Princes:
A By-Word, in the Mouth of every Subject!

Beauf. I muft commend my Nephew's Refolution:
Nor, can it be unwelcome to the King;
Whofe regal Dignity your Majefty confults.

　　　　　　　　　　　Glouceſt.

Glouceſt. Peace, *Beaufort*, Peace! —— Nor, Madam,
  think that You
(Though crown'd, with Pomp, as Queen of this fair
  Realm)
Have any Right, to cenſure my Endeavours
To ſerve, alike, my Countrey, and my King;
Whoſe Intereſts are the ſame:— Not ſacred Wedlock
Is a cloſer Tie. —— As for My Actions;
To our Sovereign Lord, the Nobles, and the Commons,
(Our legal Powers) am I accountable: ——
And, ſo is *Beaufort*; and your Favourite, *Suffolk*;
And You, my royal Dame!

Queen. Preſumptuous Man! ——

Suff. Why ſhould your Majeſty, thus, condeſcend ——

Queen. The vain Applauſes of the wretched Commons
Have ſwoln thy Heart with Pride!——

Beauf. They have, indeed.
Who has not heard the Blaſt of vulgar Breath,
Calling him *Humfrey*, the Good Duke of *Gloucester*;
Clapping their Hands, and crying with loud Voice,
Long may your royal Excellency live;
With, Heaven preſerve the Good Duke *Humfrey!* ——

Suff. No Mention of the King, in all their Tran-
  ſport:—
Duke *Humfrey* reigns!

Queen. I bluſh, my Lords,
To recollect, how gentle *Henry's* Goodneſs
Has been abus'd. ——

Glouceſt. And, Madam, *Gloucester* bluſhes:
But, not for any Guilt of His.

Queen. Moſt inſolent!——
To Whom doeſt Thou intend the Provocation?
Speak out thy Inſinuations:— We defy thee!——
But, *Gloucester*, if thou dareſt to looſe thy Tongue
Againſt my Fame, unſully'd, as the Light;
Here, by my royal Father's Life, I ſwear
Perdition on thy Head!—— More fatal Vengeance,
Than, ever, injur'd Woman did accompliſh.

Glouceſt.

Glouceft. Wherein, do I accufe your Majefty?
I anfwer, only, as to my Sovereign's Goodnefs;
Never, abus'd by Me. —— Thefe bufy Flies,
That ever feek the Sunfhine of the Court,
Will ruin Him, and You. —— I am content
To quit my Apartment in the Palace. — And,
(Whatever They, through Envy, may fuggeft)
Gloucefter was never fordidly ambitious
Of popular Applaufe. —— If, to do Juftice,
If, to protect the Commons from Oppreffion,
Be judg'd a Crime; I am, indeed, moft criminal.
And, yet; unlefs the Commons do enjoy
Their Rights; and, be indulg'd their Freedom:
In my poor Thought, the King, with all his Nobles,
Is deftitute; unable to repell
A forreign Foe; or rule in Peace, at Home.

S C E N E VIII.

Suffolk. Gloucefter. Beaufort. Queen. Buckingham.

Queen. Say, *Buckingham,* ——
Buckin. All is prepar'd.
Queen. 'Tis well. ——
Gloucefter, thy idle Speeches pafs my Ear,
As does the wafting Wind.
Beauf. Madam, you fee,
My Nephew can declaim.
Queen. By *Gloucefter's* Actions,
Will I interpret his fair-feeming Words.
Was it not He, my Lords, oppos'd my Marriage;
Which my Good Lord of *Winchefter* approv'd?
Was it not He, who fcorn'd my Father's Titles?
Of *Naples, Scicily, Jerufalem,* King! ——
Was it not *Gloucefter,* did uphold his Wife
To bear her Port above me, in the Palace?
And who, befide this Duke, in every Thing,
Has check'd my Power, and thwarted my Defires! ——

All which Indignities, when I forgive ;
May I be hooted through the Streets, like *Eleanor !*

    Glouceft. Were You unfortunate, She would not triumph.

    Queen. I fee through thy Submiffion ; miftaken Man!——

Thou doeft refign an Office, thou haft not Power,
Longer, to hold :—— Nay, dareft not hold it, longer.

    Glouceft. Not dare to hold our Office ? —— Yes ; We dare !——

Nor, will we give it up to *Reiner*'s Daughter,
Whofe whole Inheritance is empty Titles ;
Whom *Eleanor* furmounts, in every Vertue!——
See my Submiffion ? — No ; Miftaken Woman !——
Not dare ; proud *Margaret ?*—— Every Thing We dare,
That our Allegiance warrants !—— We, even, dare
To difabufe the King ;— which *Suffolk* dares not do :
Suffolk, who brought the Curfe ——

    Queen. Arreft the Traitour !

    Glouceft. Arreft the Lord Protectour ;——

    Queen. Him ;— this Inftant!——

    Glouceft. Who holds his Power, by Parliament ?——

    Queen. Yes : Seize him ! —
That Duke of *Gloucefter,* there !——

    Glouceft. Who offers
Such Violence (though, in the Prefence-Chamber)
Tempts my Sword.

    Queen. Suffolk, forbear !—— We come not, here, to combat. —

Lord *Buckingham* ; produce your Orders.

    Buckin. Your Highnefs may perufe them.

    Queen. My Lord of *Winchefter,* do You remain ;
And, bring us an Account of his Behaviour.

SCENE

SCENE IX.

Gloucefter. Beaufort. Buckingham.

Glouceft. I fee, His Majefty, hereby, commands,
That I fhould, on Sufpicion of high Treafon,
Remain confin'd to my Apartment ; 'till
His Pleafure be, farther, known.—— I obey.——
Seem not furpris'd, good Uncle: Though, You know,
This Order is illegal.—— But, We Obey.
 Beauf. The King, beft, knows the Limits of his
  Power.
With Him, you may difpute——
 Glouceft. Not, with the King ;
But, with his new Advifers.
 Buckin. Your Highnefs may obferve,
My Orders do admit of no Delay.
 Glouceft. I go.—— Uncle, good Night.
To Morrow, We may talk, in Parliament.
Mean Time, We fleep:—— If we are innocent,
We, Both, may fleep.—— Lord *Buckingham* ; my Duty
To my lov'd Sovereign. —— Alas ! He knows not,
If *Gloucefter* fhould be over-born by Faction,
Or, die of Grief ; He has not, long, to wear
His Crown. —— Once more, my reverend Uncle,
Good Night.
 Beauf. A fweet, and found Repofe, to *Gloucefter.*

SCENE X.

Beaufort.

Humfrey, farewell :—— And, when I do behold
Thy Face, again ; then, may thy Looks have Power
To blaft my Thought with Madnefs !—— To Mor-
 row,

Wilt

Wilt thou talk in Parliament?——— Thy to Morrow
I caſt into Eternity!——— But ; How?———
The Manner of the Deed lies, yet, confus'd.———
This way ;——— Or,— That :——— Ay ;— So !———

S C E N E XI.

Beaufort.   Warwick.

Warw. What ſhould detain the Lord Protectour!———
Beauf. No : ———
That will not do. ———
  Warw. He may miſtake the Hour.———
  Beauf. Ha!— What Voice?——— The Earl of
    Warwick. ———
  Warw. Lord Cardinal ! ———
'Tis ſomewhat Strange, to find You, out of Council,
At ſuch a buſy Time.
  Beauf. Perhaps, You come
To ſeek the Duke of *Gloucefter* ; now, unhappily,
Under Confinement.
  Warw. Under Confinement!———
How ? Where? Why?——— Unhappily !———
Contrivance, all ! — It muſt ; — A Plot of Thine :
Who, elſe, durſt to ———
  Beauf. Paſs on to his Apartment ;
And, He may be at Leiſure to inform you.
  Warw. A Priſoner?— The Protectour of the
    Realm !———
By what Authority?——— Say, Biſhop ;— Cardi-
    nal ! ———
  Beauf. Young, haſty *Warwick,* queſtion not thy
    Betters ;
Who owe thee no Reply.
  Warw. But, we ſhall find
A Time, and Place, to queſtion Thee,— to Purpoſe.
For, if the King, herein, has been advis'd
To ſtretch his Power, beyond the Law ; Thy Malice,
                                            Th)

Thy daring Malice, only, has betray'd him.

  Beauf. Rafh Boy, thy Menaces rife fhort of Me;
Who move within a Sphere, exalted high,
Above thy Lay-Condition! —— We love our Nephew:
And, to our beft Abilities, We ferve the King.
Adieu: —— And, learn more Reverence to Our Or-
    der.

SCENE XII.

Warwick.

  Proud, — and Rich Cardinal! — No wonder
    Thou art proud:
Thy Order can be Proud and Poor: In Shew,
Moft humble; in Heart, moft arrogant. —— The Monk,
That asks an Alms, is a proud, lazy Varlet. ——
Fie upon this Mockery!
  O, might I live to blefs the happy Day,
When *Rome*, no more, ufurps tyrannick Sway! —
Or, That deny'd; may our Defcendents fee
The Land, throughout, from Superftition free:
With Kings, who fill an independent Throne,
And know no Power, Supreme, befide their Own!

End of the Third A C T.

ACT IV. SCENE I.

York. Salisbury.

York.

BY Heaven, it makes me mad! —— The Queen
    and *Suffolk*
Govern the King; and, *Beaufort* governs Them.
   Salisb. Let them go on. —— This Act of Violence
Renders them more obnoxious: And (you find)
My Son has brought the Duke into our Measures.
   A Night's Confinement is of no Prejudice
To Him;— And, this arbitrary Proceeding
Will inflame the Commons.
   York. May their Resentment
Burst, like avenging Thunder, on the Guilty;
And wake this bigotted, uxorious King,
Lull'd in a Dream of Love, and Superstition!
   Salisb. Once more (before we see the Lord Protec-
    tour)
Beware, how you inform him of the Dutchess:
For, should He know of my Request to *Stanley*;
It might divert his Thoughts, from ——
   York. I am caution'd.
The Publick, now, must have his whole Attention.
   Salisb. If our Designs succeed; Her Banishment
May be repeal'd; and, her Accusers punish'd: ——
If otherwise; a Day, or Two, is not

A mighty Trefpafs : And, the Blame fhall reft
On Me, alone.

 York. Moft Generous, and Wife!

 Salisb. But fee ; — the Council-Chamber opens : ——
  And,

Beaufort moves this Way.—— Do you difcourfe him ;
While I confer with *Gloucefter,* 'till You come.

 York. You know, I hate him.

 Salisb. Treat him with Contempt :
And try, if, in his Rage, he can diffemble.

S C E N E. II.

York, Beaufort.

 York. So! —— Now, he aims a Smile of Treachery
  at me.

 Beauf. What ? — My right-noble Friend ; the Duke
of *York !* ——
And (or my Eye-fight fails) the Earl of *Salisbury*
Parted from you. —— Why were you not at Council ?

 York. Were we not, Both, fhut out ? ————

 Beauf. You furprife me !

 York. Am I your Mirth ? ———— I tell thee, Car-
  dinal ;
Had there been prefent, at the Board, One honeft Man,
Gloucefter had not been feifed.

 Beauf. Had I been prefent ;
What could a fingle Voice ? — And That, not much,
  regarded ?

 York. Moft profligate Diffembler ! —— { *Half*
                 { *afide.*

 Beauf. Nay, my Lord ;
Were I not fway'd, like You, by *Humfrey*'s Vertues ;
Yet, would the Ties of Blood, alone, engage me,
On all Occafions, to fupport my Nephew.

 York. The Ties of Blood!—— No, *Winchefter !* ——
  The Priefthood,
To Celibacy vow'd, are dead to all Endearments. ——

                   What

What Ties have You?——Nor conjugal, nor filial
    Love;
Nor Brotherhood, nor Parents Griefs, or Joys,
Nor Friendſhip's generous Flame, nor Sympathies
Of any Kind, affect Your Hearts!——

    Beauf. Forbear:——
I muſt not hear you, thus inveigh againſt
Your Spiritual Guides.

    York. Our mercileſs Oppreſſers!——
In all your Intereſts, ſever'd from the People,
Of worldly Wealth, and Pomp, and Power, you would
Ingroſs the Whole; And leave, to Us, the Cares,
The Servitude, the Penury, of Life:
Giving us empty Benedictions, in Exchange,
For the ſubſtantial Bleſſings, You enjoy.

    Beauf. Would you deſtroy the Authority of our
    Church?

    York. It's Tyranny.—— A heavy Yoke, impos'd
Not upon Subjects only, but on Kings!——
Should One, of Your Diſtinction, be arreſted;
Nay, an inferiour Prieſt;— And even by Law:
You, ſoon, would raiſe an Outcry, full of Tumult,
To ſhake, if not ſubvert, the eſtabliſht Throne.

    Beauf. I do intreat your Patience:——In this Affair,
I am moſt innocent.—— The Lord Protectour
And I, indeed, have had ſome Differences;
Occaſion'd, rather by Miſtakes, on both Sides,
Than Malice:— Broils, long ago, by Me
Forgotten;—— And, Your unkind Suſpicion
Of my Sincerity — recalls them,— to my Grief.

    What Jealouſy the King, now, entertains
Of Him, I cannot gueſs: But, will endeavour,
With all my beſt Perſwaſion, to remove it.

    York. I know thee, for the mortal Foe of *Glou-*
    ceſter!——
And, — but thou meditat'ſt ſome monſtrous Miſchief,
(What it may be, Time only can reveal!)
Thou would'ſt not, thus, ſmother thy Enmity,

                    To

To Me; who have mark'd thee, for the Worft of Men!

 Beauf. Opprobrious Rage! — What Hatred do I
  fhew?

 York. True Malice, rankling deep within the Heart,
Holds not Communication with the Tongue.

 Beauf. Let me refrain from Anger ftill: — Though
  York,
In his uncharitable Thoughts perfifting,
Condemn my meek Forbearance. ———

 York. In Forbearance,
Like the chill Snake, with inward Venom fraught;
That, coil'd, within the flowery Herbage lurks:
Sure Death to the unwary Tread. ———

 Beauf. Enough! ———
Nor think, the Dread of Thee, prefuming *York,*
Checks our Difpleafure. — But, we difdain to wrangle
With every peevifh Duke. ——— I, here, renounce
Thy Friendfhip! ———

 York. Thine, have I, long, renounced! ———

 Beauf. Thou haft difclos'd fuch Rancour, in thy
  Soul;
That, were I innocent, as dying Saints,
And *Gloucefter,* — not exempt from human Woes,
Should prove Unfortunate, — (Which Heaven forbid!)
Thy Malice would reflect the Blame, on Me.

 York. Beaufort; — I never lov'd thee; But; — for
  thy calm,
Thy fteady Diffimulation, — Thou art, now,
My fix'd Abhorrence! — Happy, for *Gloucefter!*
It is not in Thy Power to harm the Man,
Whofe Vertues make him reverenced through the Land.

S C E N E

S C E N E III.

Beaufort.

'Tis Time his Vertues, then, were canoniz'd :
Thofe Vertues, ever dangerous to Me! ——
It muft be done. —— The War is, now, declar'd : ——
Warwick and *York* have given us ample Warning. ——
The Duke of *Suffolk*. ——

S C E N E IV.

Beaufort. Suffolk.

Beauf. My Lord, it will be late,
Ere you can reach your Houfe. —— What, more have
    You
To fay? —— Or, know you not, You are expected
Early, to Morrow; — that you wafte thofe Hours,
Which Sleep demands?
    Suff. Why are the Friends of *Gloucefter*
Admitted to him? —— I thought, you did propofe,
By this Arreft, to difappoint their Meeting.
    Beauf. His meeting Them, at *Warwick's*. ——
    There, indeed,
His Prefence had prov'd fatal.
    Suff. Yet, methinks,
This Liberty fhould not have been allow'd.
    Beauf. I judged it otherwife : And, accordingly,
Inftructed the Centinels ; left, it might feem
Too rigorous a Proceeding, in the King.
Befide ; were his Confinement more fevere,
It might create Sufpicion ——
    Suff. Sufpicion? — Of What ?
    Beauf. A Clamour, — I would fay : —— But,
    this Day's Hurry
Disjoints my Words. ——

                                            Suff.

Suff. Here comes the Queen!—— What can it
  mean? ——

SCENE V.

Beaufort. Suffolk. Queen.

Queen. Oh, *Suffolk!* — *Winchefter!* —— I fear'd, you
  were
Retir'd to reft. ——
  Beauf. What is it, thus, alarms
Your Majefty?
  Queen. 'Tis faid, the *Londoners*
Are, All, in Uproar; —— that, they now prepare
To move, this Way; vowing, they will not Sleep,
Till they have fet their Idol-Duke at Liberty.
  Beauf. Meer harmlefs Noife; an empty Crack of
    Thunder!
  Suff. My Lord, I fear, your Counfels are too rafh.
  Beauf. Rather accufe the Rafhnefs of Your Fears.
  Queen. Is this a Time, my Lords, to move Conten-
    tion?
  Suff. To Me, I do confefs, there is, in Life no Dread
Like that of popular Fury! —— From it's Rage,
In vain we fly to Courage, or to Conduct.
  Queen. Let us, then weigh the Events, on either
    Side. ——
Suppofe, — We fhould releafe the Duke? ——
  Beauf. And, let
Our Adverfaries fee, they can defeat
Your Refolutions, by the flighteft Rumour.
Or, — grant it True: —— What happier Incident
Could we expect, to affure us of Succefs
You, Madam, can improve it, to the King:
For, — Who, but *Gloucefter*, caufes this Sedition? ——
Shall *Gloucefter* be Protectour, then?
  Queen. I fee,
His Popularity is dangerous to the State.

Beauf.

Beauf. Moft ruinous! ——And will your Majefty`
(Whofe dauntlefs Spirit is your envied Glory)
Be over-awed, by a tumultuous Rout,
To fave the Man, ———
 Queen. The Man, whom I deteft! ——
If, I but fmile on *Suffolk*; He repines :
And thinks the whole Indulgence of the Court
Due to Himfelf, alone.
 Suff. Madam, the Man,
Diftinguifh'd by Your Smiles, may boaft an Honour,
The foremoft Princes of the Earth would prize :
And, thus diftinguifh'd, I look down on *Gloucefter!*
 Beauf. I would intreat your Majefty to reft,
This Night, fecure ; and You, my good Lord *Suffolk:*
Remembring, ftill, if any Tumult fhould
Arife, to Morrow, that we all ftand firm. ———
The King, who yields to popular Commotions,
Is more the Slave, than Sovereign, of his People.
 Queen. My Lord of *Winchefter* ; I know, Your
  Thought
Muft be fatigued. —— Good Night. —— The King
  refolves,
Early, to meet the Parliament.
 Beauf. By Noon,
If I compute aright, the Power of *Gloucefter*
Ceafes. ———

S C E N E VI.

Beaufort.

 Beauf. So far, we profper, — unfufpected. ———
Now, to my Two bold Hirelings ; — Men, inur'd
To defperate Ills : Whofe Livelyhood is Rapines,
And gainfull Murders ; whom *Gloucefter*'s Power
Reduced to Want. —— They wait for my Inftructions ;
And, may fufpect me, wavering, in my Purpofe.

       S C E N E

SCENE VII.

The Lord Protectour's Apartment.

Gloucefter. York. Salisbury.

Glouceft. Not, that I fhould have given my Office
    up,
Without confulting You. —— I, rather, meant
To try the Queen, and fathom their Intentions.
    York. Your Highnefs might, as well, give up your
        Life:
And leave the King, and People to thefe Spoilers.
    Salisb. The Peers (of their high Privileges jealous)
Will, never, condefcend to hear of Bufinefs,
'Till You have taken your Seat in Parliament:
Nor, will We, affembled, fuffer your Confinement
To be prolong'd, an Hour; ere we demand
The Caufe of your Arreft. —— When you appear;
With all your wonted Energy of Speech,
Boldly, in Prefence of his Majefty
And Both the Houfes, fet forth your Innocence;
Demanding Reparation, for this Outrage.
Then, — openly affert the Power, you hold by Law;
The Truft committed to you. —— Take the King
To your Protection; — And, feclude that female
Politician: —— And, let her Paramour,
And *Beaufort*, abide the Juftice of their Peers.
    Glouceft. What fhall I fay, my Lords? — By gen-
        tler Methods,
I would fecure the Welfare of the State! ——
    York. Muft You forgive, and They offend, for ever?
    Salisb. The Nation Suffers, through your Mode-
        ration:
And Clemency, mifplaced, emboldens Traitours!
    The Wrongs, the Indignities, the bold Attempts,
            E 2   (Year

(Year after Year) level'd againſt your Perſon,
With the accumulated Inſults of this Day,
I mention not ; — ſince, You are pleas'd to o'erlook
All Injuries, but what regard your Countrey. ——
But, — if the Weal of *England* does require,
Your Enemies ſhould be ſeverely puniſh'd ;
Will *Glouceſter*, ſtill, be partial to their Crimes,
Only, becauſe They have offended Him ?

    Glouceſt. I think, my Breaſt did, never, nouriſh
      Malice. —

And yet, — ſo apt is Power to warp with Paſſion ;
And, ſo over-prone is Cenſure ; that, I wiſh
(While I diſcharge my Duty to my Countrey)
Keen-ſearching Envy might diſcern no Glimpſe
Of ſecret Vengeance, in my publick Actions.

    Salisb. Rather, my Lord, ſuſpect your Lenity ;
Your too-long Suffering : —— Leſt, it be ſaid ;
You court Applauſe, — at the Expence of Juſtice.

    York. Beaufort's and *Suffolk's* Crimes, againſt the
      State,
Are ſo enormous ; that, all honeſt Men
Will blame your Highneſs, ſhould They go unpuniſh'd.
    Has not the One (to ſpeak not half his Guilt)
By Frauds againſt the Crown, by Sale of Offices,
By Plunder from the People, and the Clergy,
Amaſs'd ſuch vaſt Exuberance of Wealth ;
That Millions, daily, curſe him, by the Name
Of the *Rich Cardinal?* —— Has not the Other ——

    Glouceſt. O, ſpeak it not! —— To what a Pitch
    of Glory
Did our Late Leader, of immortal Memory,
Build up the Nation's Proweſs ? — That (like a Py-
    ramid
Of Fire, high on a Mountain rais'd, to ſhine by
    Night)
Our Blaze of Valour drew the Admiration
Of the wide Continent ! ——

    York. Our yearly Harveſt,

Con-

Conqueft on Conqueft!—— And, the *Englifh* Name
So much revered; that every private Subject,
Who travell'd far, — was an illuftrious Stranger!

  Glouceft. Bitter Remembrance!—— O, lafting In-
    famy!——

How have We fquander'd our whole Treafure of Renown!—

Spendthrifts in Fame!— The Scorn of Thofe, We
  conquer'd!

  Salisb. And, fhall this *Suffolk* live; who gave up
    France?——

The Purchafe of our nobleft Blood!—— For Which,
Great *Henry* fought!—— And, to maintain it Ours,
Bedford wore out his Life, in fore Fatigues!

  Glouceft. I have affur'd you, by the Earl of *War-
    wick,*

Of my Compliance; fince the ufual Forms
Of Law are ineffectual.

  Salisb. When Treafons, manifeft,
Are fo contriv'd (as Treafons, often, are)
That they defy the Force of Written Laws;
Or, when the Wealth, or Dignity, of Traitours
Sets them above the Reach of Common Juftice:
Attainders are the Refuge of the State.——

S C E N E VIII.

Gloucefter. York. Salisbury. Warwick.

  Salisb. My Son,— what brings you hither, from
    your Guefts?
  Warw. A fuddain Infurrection, through the City.
  Glouceft. What prompts them to Sedition, at this
    late Hour?
  Warw. Scarce was the Warrant order'd againft You,
But it is known in the remoteft Streets.——
Murmur is rife. — All Occupation ceafes.——
The Shops are clos'd.— Mafters and Prentices,

         Vari-

Varioufly accouter'd, pour, from all Parts,
To fwell the general Tumult!—— And, now, the
    Torrent
Roars, near at Hand ; and bears upon the Palace.

    York. Let it roar on !——

    Glouceft. Oh, no! my Friends.—— Their Zeal
Is too intemperate !—— Rather, let them fhew
Their Love for Me, by Duty to their King.——
Why, this Impatience ?— Does not the Parliament
Open, to Morrow ?—— Can they not, with Me,
Wait a few Hours !—— When Kings are ill-advis'd,
Have we no Remedy, but lawlefs Force ?——
Or, think they, *Gloucefter* will uphold Rebellion ?—
Sooner, would I grow hoary, in a Prifon ;
Much fooner, die ;— than purchafe Liberty, or Life,
By Violation of the Publick Peace !

    Lord *Warwick,* I befeech you, tell them fo.——
You can prevail.— Bid them, go Home in Peace.
Greet them, from Me :— Say I am not in Danger.—
The Laws are My Protection.

    Salisb. Go, my Son :——
And, add from Me ; that, if the Lord Protectour
Be not difcharg'd, foon as the Parliament
Afiembles,——

    Glouceft. There is no Fear.——

    Salisb. However ;
Let us not over-damp their Spirits, till We
Have compafs'd our Defigns.—— In a free Govern-
    ment,
The juft Refentment of the Multitude,
Difcreetly encouraged, is of mighty Force
To aid the Patriot, and to quell the Traitour.

    Glouceft. Hafte, *Warwick* ; ere they reach the Palace-
    Gates.

    Warw. I go :— And will intreat their Patience,
    till to Morrow.

S C E N E

SCENE IX.

Gloucefter. York. Salisbury.

York. Pardon me, noble *Gloucefter*; when I fay,
Your Tendernefs, for this weak Prince, prevails
Too far. ——

Glouceft. Alas, my Lords, his weak, unactive Spirit
(Since you will fearch my Soul, to know the Caufe)
Makes me more tender of a helplefs King,
To Me bequeath'd. ———— How, are my Hopes deceiv'd!
When this fole Orphan of my royal Brother
(Scarce, yet, from Infancy advanced to Childhood)
Smil'd at the Tranfports of the applauding Crow'd,
As on the trapped Steed, that wont to bear
His Father's Manhood, Cherub-like He rode
To meet his Parliament; — Oh, what Bleffings
Did ever, Age, and Sex, and every Rank,
From Windows and high Battlements, fhower down
On godlike *Henry*'s Son!———— How did My Joy
(Flooding my Eyes, and confpiring with the People)
Prognofticate, and promife to the Nation,
The Wifdom, Juftice, Prowefs, of my Brother,
Should fpring afrefh, and flourifh, in his Heir!
York. While You furvive; and will exert your juft
Authority: The Nation bears the Difappointment.
Salisb. Nor, will they endure it, long, on other
Terms.
Glouceft. To each of You, kind Heaven has granted
Sons,
Born to prolong your Vertues!—— Wherefore, was
that
Felicity deny'd to *Henry*'s Memory?——
Or, muft One Generation pafs; or, more;

E 4

Ere

Ere Providence determines to renew
His Likeneſs; and diſtinguiſh, once again,
The Blood of *Lancaſter*, and *England*'s Glory!
　Salisb.　Why was the Education of our Prince in-
　　truſted
To *Beaufort?* With whom, the Metropolitan
Of *York* conſpir'd, to enfeeble his tender Mind
With Legendary Tales, and falſe Devotion;
That They might rule him, in his riper Years.
　York.　When Superſtition (Bane of manly Vertues!)
Strikes Root within the Soul; it over-runs,
And kills, the Power of Reaſon.

S C E N E　X.

Glouceſter.　York.　Salisbury.　Warwick.

　Glouceſt.　What Tidings, now?——
　Warw.　The Tumult is appeas'd.
　Glouceſt.　*Warwick,*—— thy free-giving Hand; thy
　　Table,
Open to All; thy affable Deportment;
Thy pleaſing Wit;—— (Endearing Qualities!)
Conciljate to Thee, daily, ſuch Good Will,
From all Degrees of Men: That, I foreſee,
Thy Influence will prevail, throughout the Realm.
　York.　Left we intrude too far upon the Night;
Your Highneſs will appoint our Shares of Buſineſs:
That there be no Confuſion, in our Meaſures.
　Glouceſt.　My 'Lords,—— when I am juſtified; Let
　　Salisbury
(Whoſe Gravity beſpeaks Attention) open,
In general Terms, the heinous Crimes, long practiced
Againſt the King, and State: And dwell upon
The melancholy Proſpect, now, before us.
　Salisb.　I take My Part.
　Glouceſt.　Then; let the Duke of *York*
Unfold each Circumſtance of *Suffolk*'s Treaſon.

York.

York. Agreed.

Warw. And, leave the Cardinal to Me. ——
Methinks, I ſee vain *Suffolk* lower his Creſt : ——

York. And *Wincheſter's* red, fiery Eyes betray
The Virulency of his feſtering Soul.

Saliſb. But, We forget your Highneſs ; whoſe Eloquence,
Strengthen'd with Probity, ————

Glouceſt. In the Debate,
Oft' as the Nation's Danger, and the King's,
Shall come in View, will I riſe up to ſpeak ;
And ſhew my forward Zeal, at leaſt, to reſcue
The King, and Nation, truſted to my Care.

Saliſb. Thus, then, will We inſtruct our Friends ;
who wait,
Impatient, for Our final Reſolutions.

Glouceſt. Yet, ere we part ; grant One Requeſt.

Warw. You may
Command your Friends.

Glouceſt. My Lords, I offer not
To extenuate the Guilt of *Beaufort* ; nor, am I
Ignorant of his up-lifted Pride,
Which renders him moſt hatefull to the Nobles :
But ſtill, this hated, this obnoxious Prelate, ——
Is he not my Uncle ? —— Then for My Sake,
Spare the Remainder of his Life. —— His Father
Was a moſt worthy Prince ; and his late Brother,
The Duke of *Exceſter,* a wiſe, a learned,
And an upright Counſellour.

York. If he muſt live ;
Let him have no Abode within the Palace.

Warw. Confine him to his Dioceſs, for Life ;
That he may not infeſt the Court : Nor, hencefor-
ward,
Embroil the State.

Saliſb. Nor, muſt he hold
A Seat, in Parliament : —— For, what have We
To do with Cardinals ? Whoſe whole Allegiance

The

The See of *Rome* uſurps.

   Glouceſt. Nay, more; my Lords:
Let his ill-gotten Wealth (Wherewith, he hopes
To buy the Papal Crown) be forfeited.
   On theſe Conditions, let my Uncle live; —
And die, in Peace.
   Salisb. At Your Deſire, then, let him
Find that Mercy, he merits not.
   York. A Mercy,
Were You in need of it, He ne'er would grant.
   Glouceſt. Though old in Vice; Retirement and
      Reflection
May, by Degrees, ſubdue his Heart to Vertue.
   Warw. Is there Aught, more; before we leave your
      Highneſs?
   Glouceſt. My Lords; — Commend me to our Aſ-
      ſembled Friends:
And give them full Aſſurance, in My Name;
That, as in War, the Fear of Death ne'er drove me
From Perils of the Field: I will, to Morrow,
Shew equal Reſolution, in the Senate.
Nor, ſhall the Dread of Envy, or Detraction,
Nor, yet, the Frowns, nor the Conſpiracies,
Of deſperate Wicked Men, abate that Ardour,
With which Your friendly Counſels make me glow
To ſerve, at once, our Countrey, and our King!

S C E N E XI.

Glouceſter.

With Mildneſs, have I exercis'd my Power: ——
But, — when the Times require Severity;
Forbearance is Injuſtice. ——— *Beaufort*'s Life, —
If he employs it well, is well preſerv'd. ———
Sore with the Provocations of the Day,
I have (I fear) with too great Bitterneſs
Reproach'd his Age: —— But, let me not lie down,
                  In

In Wrath ; — Nor rife, in Enmity : — Though,
    Malice
May keep Him waking, on his Pillow. —— Oh,
    Eleanor ; —
My Bed, alas, without Thee, is folitary, —
As is the Grave ! —— But, Sleep weighs down my
    Eye-lids ;
And Nature, wearied, fummons me to Reft.—— { *Going in.*
Angels, defend me ! —— What do I fee ? — My Un-
    cle ? ——
And , in his Hand, a Dagger ; —— a bloody Dag-
    ger ! ——
Away, Illufion ! — Phantom of the Brain ! ——
My Senfes drouze ; — and, Fancy mocks my Rea-
    fon ! ——
It is beyond my wonted Hour. —— Then, — wel-
    come
Kind Sleep ; Renewer of our daily Life :
Till, Death clofing our Eyes for ever from the World,
We wake to One, Eternal, Day of Blifs !

S C E N E XII.

Beaufort.

At length, I find the Stilnefs, I have wifh'd. ——
The Mutineers are pacified : The Friends
Of *Gloucefter* are retir'd : The Centinels,
O'erpower'd with Wine, Sleep a dead Sleep. — The
    Hour,
Paft Midnight, waftes in the Glafs. —— Soon the
    Bell,
That parcels Time, will give the appointed Signal :
The Minute for the Deed. —— Hark ! — Was That,
    a Groan ? —
Again ? —— The hollow-whirling Wind. —— O, lull
    the Duke

                              To

To his eternal Reſt ! ——— Yet ; — I feel Somewhat,
Bids me forbear ; — and pleads, within, for Mer-
cy. ———
Idle Remorſe ! ——— What though He be my Ne-
phew ? ———
Were he my Father : — Muſt I imbitter Life ;
Quit all my Hopes ; — and forfeit my Ambiti-
on ? ———
Did he not, Twice, attempt my Overthrow ? ———
And, will he, exaſperated as he is,
Spare me, to Morrow ? ——— Then, — Self-Defence,
Nature's firſt Law, acquits me, to my Self. ———
He makes Me wretched : ——— I ſet Him at Eaſe. ———
What Injury ? ——— He leaves no helpleſs Orphan :
And, to his Wife he is, allready, dead. ———
And ; What is Loſs of Life ? — A Loſs, we never
Regret. ——— Would it were done ! — And, I
a ſleep ! ———
It ſtrikes ! ——— The Stroke of unrelenting Fate ! ———
Sleep, *Humfrey* ; ſleep ! ——— The Period of Thy Cares,
And Mine, is come. ——— Ha ! — What warning
Voice ? Whence ? ———
Methinks, I hear a Voice cry ; *Glouceſter*, awake ! —
Who comes ? ———

S C E N E XIII.

Beaufort. Two Ruffians.

1. *Ruffian.* Lord Cardinal. ———
Beauf. Ay. ——— Tread ſoft. ——— Heard you no
Noiſe ?
2. *Ruffian.* The Bell.
Beauf. No other Sound ?
1. *Ruffian.* Not any ; my good Lord.
Beauf. No Noiſe, before you enter'd ?
1. *Ruffian.* None at all.

Beauf.

Beauf. It may be fo. —— And yet, it hollow'd
   loud !——

Imaginary Terrours ! — Hence ! —— Is Age
So quick of Hearing ? ———— Come, my Friends :
Are you prepared ?

   2. *Ruffian.* So bent on Vengeance ;
That We think, Stifling is too mild a Death.

   Beauf. No : —— No Bloodfhed !——

   1. *Ruffian.* Does he fleep found ?

   Beauf. No labouring Man more found. ——
But, — you muft ufe main Force.

   1. *Ruffian.* We know his Strength.

   Beauf. There lies the Door.

   2. *Ruffian.* Come : — Set the Lanthorn.

   Beauf. But ;
Be fure, you leave no Signs of Violence : ——

   2. *Ruffian.* None.

   Beauf. And, lay the Bed ; — and place the Pillows,
   after. ——

Turn the Lock gently ; — very gently ! —— So. ——
   Can Murder be a crying Offence ; and Heaven
Permit fuch Fellows, daily, to traffick in it ? —
Or, is it human Laws, alone, confpire
To make it Criminal ? —— But, hold ! —— 'Tis do-
   ing. ——

He ftruggles ! —— Now ; — all your Might : — Dif-
   patch ! —— No Refpite !——

Force : —— Wretches ; more Force ! —— Weigh on
   his Breaft. ——

Smother that Groan ! —— His Mouth ; — his Noftrils : Quick ! ——

Daftardly Mifcreants ! —— Still I hear him breathe.——

Finifh, at once ! —— Oh, 'tis a tedious While ! ——

So. —— Now, he lies quiet. — Yes. —— At laft, 'tis
   over ! ——

Examine ; — carefully : —— Feel every Pulfe. ——

Leave

Leave not One doubtfull Token. —— Quite extinguiſh
Life ! —— —— Is it done ?
    1. *Ruffian.* To all Intents.
    Beauf. Quite dead ?
    2. *Ruffian.* We anſwer for it.
    Beauf. Yet ; —— I ſee no Blood
Upon your Hands ! ——
    2. *Ruffian.* You did injoin us. ——
    Beauf. True ! ——
I had forgot. —— And, have you ſmooth'd the Bed ?
    1. *Ruffian.* We have : — And, drawn the Curtains,
    round : ——
    2. *Ruffian.* And, laid him,
With his Face upward.
    Beauf. Right ! —— —— Away ! —— The private
    Door is open. ——

S C E N E. XIV.

Beaufort.

How ſoon —— Liſt ! —— Does he not ſtir ? ——
    No. ——
The Breath of Life is mixt with common Air ! ——
While *Gloucefter* liv'd, nor *Henry*'s Death, nor *Bedford*'s,
Did avail ; —— Three Nephews, born to thwart
    me ! ——
Henceforth ; — Anxiety, adieu ! —— Look forward,
    Beaufort !
Nor, waſte One Thought, idly, to recollect
What cannot be recall'd. —— And yet ; — Who
    knows ? ——
Hence, childiſh Fears ! —— ——
The Queen and *Suffolk* wiſh him dead. —— No Blood
Is ſpilt : — Nor, livid Stains of Poiſon taint his
    Bowels. ——

What

What Proof of Murder, then ? ―― It will be ∫aid,
He, ∫leeping, died (as Many Men have died)
And, deem'd a Mercy ; or, perhaps, a Judgment ;
As Prejudice inclines. ―― And, Who ∫hall dare
To ca∫t, on Us, a Blemi∫h of Su∫picion ? ――
Then, *Beaufort* ; — re∫t, ∫ecure ? ―― Repute thy Self,
Free from all Guilt ; ∫ince Thou ha∫t prov'd Succe∫sfull :
Nor, vainly think, there can be Rea∫on to repent.――
The Sting of Guilt is — but the Fear of Puni∫hment !

End of the Fourth A C T.

ACT V. SCENE I.

Queen.   Suffolk.

Queen.

OH, *Suffolk*; may this Morning prove auspicious.!
    That my fond Wishes, seconded by Power,
May lavish Honours on the Man, who merits
Higher Distinction, than *England*'s Crown can give.

Suff. And, may your *Suffolk* live to serve, to admire,
To adore, the Queen ; whose Favour is my whole Ambition!

Queen. This flattering Hope, alone, emboldens me
In all my Attempts (successfull, hitherto)
To break the Authority of this Protectour.

Suff. Madam, ere Noon, your Wishes are accomplish'd.

Queen. And yet, — there hangs a Cloud upon my
Hopes ! —
And my Heart bodes ——

Suff. Let Me partake your Fears.

Queen. But ; — wherefore should a Dream disquiet
me ?

Suff. Wherefore, indeed! — Dreams, pleasing or
displeasing,
Are, only, Shadows of our waking Thoughts. ——
But, here comes *Beaufort.*

SCENE

SCENE II.

Queen. Suffolk. Beaufort.

Queen. Lord Cardinal, Good Morrow.

Beauf. Your Majefty wears not the Smiles, this Day
Requires : —— This long-expected Day.

Suff. A Dream
Has overcaft her wonted Chearfulnefs.

Queen. A Dream,
So very wild ! —— And yet, fo powerfull, it wrought ;
That, from my Slumbers, I awoke difordet'd.
Methought I faw a hunted Stag take Refuge
In a wide Stream ; — not unlike the *Thames :* —
And, when I look'd again ; That Stag — was *Suf-
folk !* —
Again, I flumber'd : — When another Dream
Sets *Beaufort* in my View ; — befmear'd with Blood ! —
And *Warwick,* — crying Murder, through the Pa-
lace ! —
What I faw, after, was — embattled Armies ! —
The King, dethroned ! — My Self, a Wanderer ! —
And *York ;* — Yet foon, it was not *York ;*
But, a frefh-blooming Youth, who wore the Crown !

Beauf. This, only, fhews ; your Majefty is anxious
For the King's Honour, and Safety of your Friends.
I, my felf, did dream, *Gloucefter* was taken Speech-
lefs ! ——
Muft it, therefore, be fo ? —— Or, does it not
Proceed from the Concern of Yefterday ?
When, there was Caufe to dread his Power of Speech !

Queen. Then, — let thefe Vifions pafs. —— But,
have you heard
Of laft Night's Tumult ?

Beauf. Nothing. —— I went to Reft.

Queen. The Duke of *Suffolk* brought the Account,
this Morning.

F

Suff.

Suff. Midnight Sedition! —— Of which I mean
  to speak
In Parliament.

  Beauf. Moſt fortunate Event! ——

  Queen. As it has prov'd. ——

  Beauf. Does the King know it?

  Queen. He does: And, is determin'd.

  Beauf. But, is he ready?

  Queen. By this Time, his Robes are on. ——

  Beauf. For, — if the Duke's Confinement be pro-
  long'd,
Till the Day wears; the Commoners and Peers
Will clamour to releaſe him, ere we can paſs
A Vote to make his Office void.

  Suff. Madam,
That Vote ſecur'd; We have reduced your Foe.

  Queen. I ask no more. —— Kind Fortune, aid us,
  now! ——
And, think not, *Glouceſter*, We (howe'er incens'd)
Would let Reſentment looſe, againſt thy Life. ——
Be Duke of *Glouceſter*, ſtill! — But not Protectour!

S C E N E III.

The Lord Protectour's Apartment.

Warwick.   Eleanor.

  Elean. All-gracious Heaven be prais'd, that I once
  more,
Shall ſee my Lord! ———

  Warw. Before the Day ſhall cloſe,
You, Both, ſhall ſee your Enemies, cover'd
With Confuſion! —— But, Madam, you have promis'd,
Not to detain him, on this important Morning.

  Elean. Miſtruſt me not. — My Reaſon ſhall o'er-rule
My fond Affection!

                                              Warw.

Warw. We kept him, late, from Reſt.

Elean. Perhaps, my Lord, He is not, yet, awake:——
And, it might be too ſuddain a Surpriſe,
Were I to draw his Curtain.

Warw. Then, let Me
Prepare him.

Elean. Gently, *Warwick,* wake my Love:
And let the Muſick of His Voice invite me to him.
O, from thy lonely Bed, my *Gloucester,* riſe:
And, may We, never more, lie down, aſunder!——
How have I watch'd, the live-long Night!—— How, chid
The tardy Morning!—— —— —— Oh, my Heart
liſtens!——
Not, yet?—— ——

Warw. Diſtraction! Horrour! Ruin!—— Murder!

Elean. Oh, my Terrour!—— What Murder; *War-*
wick?—— Where?

Warw. There; Madam!—— Horrid Murder!——

Elean. Kill me not!——
Say!——

Warw. Never more, ſhall you behold Him, living!

Elean. Whom?——

Warw. *Gloucester;* your Husband!—— The Protectour!

Elean. Say it not!—— 'Tis the Power of
Sleep!—— Let Me——

Warw. Madam, forbear!—— You muſt not ſee——

Elean. I muſt!——
I will!——

Warw. It is a Sight, will blaſt——

Elean. Let go!——
He ſhall awake!——   [*Goes in.*]

Warw. Oh, for the Voice of Thunder!
To ſhake this guilty Palace!—— To deſtroy
The Murderers!—— To ſtrike the Terrour, wide!
But, ſee the widow'd Dutcheſs!—— The Picture of
Heart-wringing Anguiſh!—— O, powerfull Affliction!

That

That neither Tears, nor Language, give it Utter-
    ance !——

  Elean. Cold!—— Quite cold!—— And ghaft-
    ly !——

O, welcome, Death !—— —— ——

  Warw. She faints !— She dies !— What Suc-
    cour ? —

Afflicted *Eleanor !* — Live !—— Live, to fee

The fpeedy Vengeance, We exact for *Gloucefter !*

The Woe, in Store for *Margaret, Beaufort, Suffolk !*

  Elean. Oh —— —— ——

  Warw. Deep-finking Sorrow !——

  Elean. Where is my *Gloucefter ?*——

O, lay me by him !——

  Warw. No :—— I cannot let you ——

  Elean. Muft I not be allow'd to live, nor die, with
    him ?——

Malice fhall not divorce me from his Grave !

  Warw. I do befeech you, Madam, to confider——

  Elean. I do :— I know my Lofs :— I feel my
    Affliction !——

  Warw. I feel it, too !— for You ; my felf ; the
    Nation !

  Elean. Why ? — Why, are there Calamities, in Life,

We cannot bear ? — That tempts us — to arraign —

Yet, — will I not.— Thou righteous Power, compaf-
    fionate

My Weaknefs !—— Authour of all Being ; — if Thou

Haft call'd Him, hence ;— O, teach me Refigna-
    tion !——

But, — if my *Gloucefter* is bereft of Life,

Through black Confpiracy ; — reveal the Murder !

  Warw. Madam, You muft not, yet, be feen. ——
    My Houfe

Is near. — My Wife will fhare in your Affliction :

While I inform the King and Parliament

Of *Gloucefter's* Fate ; and, edge the Sword of Juftice!

S C E N E

S C E N E IV.

The Scene shifts back again.

Queen.

'Tis a full Parliament! — And, big with Expecta-
    tion! ——
And, allready, do the inquisitive Multitude
Begin to gather! —— Should the Protectour's Followers
Out-number us ; — Or, should they know the Summs,
We have distributed : —— The King may be
Prevail'd on, to retract his Speech. —— O, *Henry* ;
That I could give thee a Portion of My Spirit! ——

S C E N E V.

Queen. Beaufort.

Queen. O, *Winchester!* — I am perplex'd ; — I
    fear! —
Beauf. Madam, I hasten'd to prevent your Fears. —
Queen. Why do you quit your Seat ? — Say! —
    What Occasion ? —
Has the King spoke ? ——
Beauf. Be more compos'd.
Queen. Resolve me! ——
Beauf. He would have spoke ; — when, a suprizing
    Rumour
Was circled round, — of the Protectour's Death! ——
Queen. Of *Gloucester's* Death ? — It cannot be! —
    And yet,
I, almost wish it may! ——
Beauf. A frequent Murmur
(As of Bees disturb'd within their Hives) rose
On a suddain! —— And the deep Concern,
In all his Friends, gives seeming Credit to it.

Queen.

Queen. Some Stratagem! —— But, were it true ;
   I dread
This hafty Death! —— Who knows what may be
   faid ? ——
   Beauf. We may expect, our Enemies will caft out
Malicious Whifpers.
   Queen. Ay, *Beaufort !* —— And, I wifh,
He had not been confin'd.
   Beauf. Thus, human Forefight
Is, ever, blind to the Decrees of Heaven !
   Queen. He is fo lov'd! —— fo much the Worfhip
   of the People ;
I apprehend a thoufand Mifchiefs ! ——
   Beauf. Faction
May rage, a While. —— Let Us betray no Fear :
But, bold in Innocence, confront Detraction !
   Queen. Back, to your Seat, my Lord ; and watch
   the Motions ——
Yet, ftay ! — Here, comes the Duke of *York.* ——

S C E N E VI.

Queen. Beaufort. York.

   Queen. O, tell me ! ——
Say, noble *York,* ——
   Beauf. Alafs, my Nephew ! —— Is he
Departed ? ——
   York. Murder'd ! ——
   Beauf. Murder'd ? ——
   Queen. Heaven forbid ! ——
Murder'd ? —— By Whom ? —— And, in the Palace !
   York. Yes : ——
Barbaroufly, murder'd ! —— Bafely, in his Bed !
   Beauf. How ? ——By Whom ? ——What Affurance
   of the Fact ?
   York. Concurring Circumftances ! ——

                             Queen.

Queen. Speak them, then!

York. The hafty Summons of this Parliament:
The Banifhment of *Eleanor*: His Confinement:
The Imprifoning his Servants: ——

Queen. Pardon me,
My Lord; if, in all, you urge fo vehemently,
I can difcern no Circumftance of Murder.

Beauf. This is a Tale! — A Plot, to raife Rebellion! ——

Queen. Give plainer Tokens, *York*! —— Have you examin'd
The Body?

Beauf. Is there any Blood upon the Sheets?

Queen. Make Proof! — What Marks of Violence appear?

York. O, Madam; many Witneffes, with Me,
Have feen, have read, the Characters of Murder!
Where Sicknefs kills, oft' have I feen the Corfe
Of afhy Semblance; meagre; pale; and bloodlefs:
The darken'd Eyes, in-funk; the Nofe, comprefs'd.
But, the Duke's Face is black; and full of Blood!
His Eye-Balls, farther out, than when he liv'd;
Staring, full-ghaftly; like a ftrangled Man!
His Noftrils, ftretch'd with ftrugling! His Mouth, a-gafp
For vital Breath! His ruffled Hair, up-rear'd!
His Hands, a-broad difplay'd; as One, that grafp'd,
And tugg'd for Life; and was fubdued by Force!

Beauf. Your Majefty fees, This is concerted Malice! ——

Queen. Treafon, againft the King! —— As, who fhould fay,
He fign'd a Warrant for his Uncle's Murder.

Beauf. *York* is not ignorant, that Many die,
Without the Mercy of a timely Warning! ——
Do we not, daily, petition againft fuddain Death? —
Or,—may not *Gloucefter*, confcious of fome Guilt,
Have taken Poifon? —— But; produce the Murderer!

York.

York. Thou may'ft remember; there is a Prelate, living,
Once, placed an Ambufh for his Life. ——
   Beauf. 'Tis falfe! ——
I clear'd my felf of that unworthy Charge,
Long ago:—When our moft gracious Sovereign
(May he not rue the Day!) made Thee a Duke;
In Token of his Joy, that *Beaufort* did forgive
This dear, departed, Man; then, my Accufer.

SCENE VII.

Queen. Beaufort. York. Warwick.

Warw. Why do I find you here, my Lord? ——
   Know you not
The Protectour's Enemies?——
   Queen. But, not his Murderers!
   Warw. One, I anfwer for!
   Queen. Prefumptuous *Warwick!*
More infolent, than *York!*
   Beauf. His Sycophant!
The Creature of his Smiles! —— Now, to be tame,
Would argue Guilt. —— Madam, I do pronounce
The Duke of *York,* a Traitour, by Defcent! ——
   York. There fpoke the Fiend! The Father of De-
   traction! ——
   Warw. The Murderer of *Gloucefter!* ——
   Queen. Malicious Outrage! ——
   Beauf. Slight Boy! — We fet, at Nought, what
   Thou can'ft fay.
But, that afpiring Duke (whom thou doeft eccho)
Thinks, this a Time, to manifeft his Treafon.
   York. Thou common Spoiler! — Doeft Thou talk
   of Treafon?
   Beauf. The Lord Protectour, dead; My Life is
   fought:
That *Henry* (fole-furvivin *Lancafter*)

                 Left

Left deftitute ; the hated Name of *York*
May thrive, — may tyrannize, in Ufurpation !
  Queen. 'Tis manifeft !
  Warw. How Guilt would fain evade ——
  Beauf. With him do both the *Nevils* (profufe *Warwick,*
And fubtle *Salisbury*) joyn, ——
  Warw. Blood-thirfty Man ! ——
  Queen. Yes ! — It is evident, you all confpire !——
What, elfe, fhould prompt you to be, thus, audacious ?
Thus, to arraign his venerable Age ?
A Bifhop ! — Cardinal ! — Uncle to your King !
  Beauf. And, fhall the Church, you wound through
    Me, not cenfure ! ——
O, Religion ! ——
  Queen. *Beaufort,* with Me ! ——
But ; — fee, you prove your Scandal : — Or, your
    Heads
Shall pay the Forfeit !
  Warw. I expect no Favour. ——

SCENE VIII.

York. Warwick.

  York. Your Grief, for this ill-fated Duke, tranfports you
Beyond the Bounds of Prudence.
  Warw. Fear it not. ——
Though, for a Vengeance, horrid as the Deed,
I could grow defperate ! — Could delight to torture—
  York. What Evidence ? —— That You, fo boldly
    venture
To charge the Cardinal !
  Warw. My Father bade me do it.
'Tis *Beaufort's* Guilt, he faid : — Make hafte, my Son !
Divulge it to the People ! — Cry, Bloody *Beaufort !*—
And leave the Proof, in Parliament, to Me.
  York. Inhuman Cardinal ! ——
  Warw. But, fee ; — my Father.

                 SCENE

SCENE IX.

York. Warwick. Salisbury.

York. Say, *Salisbury*; — is it *Beaufort* ?
Salisb. Yes! —— I shall
Produce the Two Assassins, he employ'd.
    York. Can such Impiety dwell so near the Altar!
But, *Salisbury*; How ——
    Salisb. Deep-wounded with Remorse ;
Dreading a Discovery ; and, hoping Pardon ;
One has, to Me, confess'd : —— But, more, at better
    Leisure.
    I must inform you, now ; The King's Affliction,
Who weeps, who droops, who sickens, on his Throne ;
The Indignation (mixt with general Mourning)
In all the Peers, and Commoners, of Note ;
The Fury of the People, rending the Air for Ven-
    geance ;
Have strook such Terrour through the Foes of *Glou-
cester,*
That, daring not to oppose our warm Resentments,
We have, already, speeded far in Justice!
    Warw. We must have Rigour, Sir ! ——
    Salisb. And shall! —— But, hear me.
Suffolk is sentenced into Banishment :
The Queen, to be remov'd, far distant, from the Pa-
    lace : ——
    York. But ; that vile *Winchester* ! ——
    Warw. Mark, where he comes.

SCENE

S C E N E X.

York. Warwick. Salisbury, Beaufort.

Beauf. Alas, my Lords! — Why am I, thus de-
famed? ——
Is not my Nephew's unexpected Death
Sufficient Weight of Grief, to bow me down?
An ample Suffering, to appeafe all Enmity?
But you muft load, — but you muft perfecute,
My Age, my Dignity, my facred Office,
With Infamy fo black, — Sufpicion of fuch Guilt,
As, Heaven can teftify, my Soul abhorrs!
   Warw. Nothing, thy Soul abhorrs; but Truth and
    Vertue!
   York. Laft Night, remember, *Beaufort*, I foretold
Some monftrous Mifchief, brooding in thy Breaft!
   Warw. Did'ft thou imagine, the Eye of Heaven
    would wink
At fuch a Deed! ——
   York. A Crime, unparallell'd!
A Murder, that fets Nature at Defiance!
   Beauf. You are young Men; yet, Strangers to
    Compaffion:
But, *Salisbury* is more weigh'd; more flow to Cenfure.
With Him, I may expoftulate; to Him reveal
My penitent Sorrow; though late, not lefs fincere.
   Why did I liften to the Queen and *Suffolk?*
Why did their fpecious Arguments feduce me?
Oh, that They never had confin'd my Nephew! ——
Unthinking, that I was! — Not to forefee,
The Violence of their unlawfull Love
Might tempt them to confpire ——
   Salisb. Go, *Beaufort;* go! ——
Thou doeft not leffen, but enhance, thy Guilt!

They

They were seduced by Thee: Thine is the Murder! ——
And (if Thy flinty Heart can feel Compunction)
Know, *Gloucester* interceded for Thy Life!
Made it his last Request, to spare his Uncle;
Enforced it with such Tenderness, that We
Consented.

Beauf. Do I not know, He was all Goodness! ——
How shall I bear the Loss! —— Oh, how lament
His hard, untimely, Fate!

Salisb. Thy black Contrivance! ——

Beauf. Then, I perceive, *Salisbury* is bent on Mischief!

Salisb. On Justice! ——

Beauf. I appeal thee, then! ——

Salisb. To Morrow! ——

Beauf. This very Day! ——

Salisb. The Lords have other Business, ——

Beauf. To Morrow, then! ——

Salisb. When, in the Presence of the Peers,
Thou shalt turn pale, and tremble, at the Sight ——

Beauf. Of *Gloucester!* — say'st Thou?

Salisb. Of the Two bold Ruffians, ——

Beauf. Curse on thy Tongue! — Thy penetrating
Thought! —

Warw. His Guilt begins to work. ——

York. It shakes his Soul!

Beauf. What Ruffians; *Nevil!* — Who? —— I am
ensnar'd! ——
Have you procur'd false Witnesses? — Or, must you
Be allow'd a Day, to seek out Perjury? —— ——
Daring Impiety! — Where will it end?
When holy Dignities are vilified!

Salisb. Presuming Insolence of *Rome*'s Authority! —
You think, that, with Impunity, You may
Offend against the Civil Power.

Beauf. I did it not.

Salisb. Deliberate Cruelty! ——

Beauf.

Beauf. They diſobey'd me, then. ——
I ſaid, No Violence ; No Bloodſhed.

Saliſb. I know it.

Beauf. I ſaid it not. — Thou could'ſt not hear
me. ——
But, I perceive your deep-concerted Malice : —
And, if I ſtir not Vengeance up ; — may Heaven
Deny me Mercy, when I need it moſt !

S C E N E XI.

York. Warwick. Salisbury.

Salisb. A direfull Imprecation !

Warw. Did you obſerve
His Reaſon ſtagger ?

Saliſb. I did.

York. That Men ſhould dare
To do, what done, muſt make the Doer wretched !

Saliſb. We, yet, ſhall wring his Conſcience ; till he
prays
For that ſweet Mercy, he has, now, renounced !
But ; — I inform'd you of the Queen, and *Suf-
folk.* ——
To *Eleanor,* the King has ſent his kind Condoleance :
Her Sentence is revok'd ; and immediate Proſecution
Order'd, againſt her infamous Accuſers.

Warw. But, — what Redreſs, for ſuffering *England?*

Salisb. *York* is deſign'd to be, what *Glouceſter* was.
But ; We muſt to our Seats, before They adjourn ;
And move, that *Beaufort's* Crime may be adjudg'd, to
Morrow.

S C E N E

S C E N E XII.

Queen.

I know not what to think! —— All is Confusion! ——
The King detain'd; and *Suffolk*, so long, absent:
Duke *Humfrey's* suddain Death; the Confidence
Of *York*, and *Warwick*; the madding Populace;
My evil-boding Dream: —— Each Circumstance
Grows black, within my Thought; and turns to
    Horrour!
  Some One dispell my Fears! ——

S C E N E XIII.

Queen. Buckingham.

Queen. O, *Buckingham*,
Thou comest, in Time, to save me from Distraction!
  Buckin. I come, the Witness of a Parliament,
Enrag'd! ——
  Queen. Have they attainted him? —— Is he, then,
Gone to Confinement? —— That I see him not! ——
Resolve me, as to *Suffolk!* —— Oh, I know it! ——
But, —— if I live, They shall not have their Will! ——
The King shall not be aw'd! — He shall release
  him. —
Fly, *Buckingham*: — Tell him, the Queen determines
To set him free!
  Buckin. How, alas! shall I inform you,
That on the first Alarm (ere, yet, his Exile
Was decreed) ——
  Queen. His Exile? —— But, he shall not go! ——
Though, Twenty Times, they voted him, to Exile;
As often would I frustrate their Resolves! —
  Buckin. Madam; — dismay'd, He fled!
  Queen. How! — Fled? —— Is he, then, gone? —
                           Persi-

Perfidious Man !——— Have I confided in him ;
Heap'd Honours on him ; ſtudied his Promotion : —
And, would he not, a Moment, ſtay his Flight,
To bid Adieu !———

Buckin. Did you but know the Whole ;———
You would compaſſionate, not blame, the Duke !———

Queen. I ſhould deteſt him, more !——— There is
   no Faith
In Man !——— Excuſe him not.——— Not ſtay, to
   thank me ? ;—
Not, once, adviſe with me ?——— Did the Wretch fear,
I would betray him ?——— Or, does he imagine,
I have no Power ?— No Senſe of Gratitude ? —
No Reſentment ?——— ——— But ; I will bring him
   back !———
Yes !— I will call the Traitour, home !——— Re-
   proach him,
To his Face !— Diſgrace him !— Meditate his
   Ruin ! —
Joyn with his Foes !— And, give him up, to
   Death !——— —
Of This, — aſſure him, when you write.
   And now, my Lord, return, to aſſiſt our Friends :
And, by your firm Adherence to our Intereſts,
Merit the Favour, forfeited by *Suffolk.*

Buckin. I could acquit him, to your Majeſty ;———
But that, I fear, Alas———

Queen. Acquit him, then !

Buckin. O, hear with Patience, what you, ſoon,
   muſt hear !
   Dreading, the People's Rage ; he ſtrove to eſ-
   cape :———
But, — far, he row'd not, down the *Thames* ; when,
   ſome
Of the diſtracted Multitude (vowing Revenge,
On *Gloucester's* Murderers) attack'd his Barge !———

Queen. And, how has he eſcap'd ?

Buckin. And murder'd him !———

Queen.

Queen. Support me! ——

Buckin. Oh, call up all your Refolution ! — fhew
Your Fortitude ! —— And be not overcome ! ——
Or, We are loft ; — Your Self is loft : — Quite
　　ruin'd !—
Your Enemies will catch at this Advantage,
To eftrange you from the King ; — to take your Life !

Queen. My Life ! —— It is imbitter'd ! —— Let
　　them take it ! ——
I am, allready, loft ! —— Eftranged from Happi-
　　nefs ! ——
Regardlefs of my Self; what Concern have I
For others ?—— Perifh, who will ! —— —— Alafs,
I rave !—— The Sport offrantick Paffion ! —— ——
Yet, — *Buckingham* ; mifconftrue not my Weaknefs :
It is, all Gratitude ! —— ——
To *Suffolk,* do I owe my Greatnefs ! ——
To *Suffolk,* I unbofom'd every Care ! ——
My Crown, without him, is a glittering Burden !
　O, Dear-bought, late, Experience ! ——. *Gloucefter,*
　　dead,
Is more my Foe, more powerfull, than living !

Buckin. Supprefs your Grief : —— See, *York* and
　　Salisbury. — Try
If, on Them you can prevail : While I
Difpofe the King —— ——

S C E N E XIV.

Queen. York. Salisbury.

York. Where is the hatefull Criminal ?
Salisb. In his Apartment ;
Seiz'd with a violent, delirious, Fever.
York. Obferve the Queen.
Queen. My Lords, I fear, I am to blame.——
Beaufort's Counfels
Have prov'd pernicious to the King.

Salib.

Salisb. And, Madam, Yours
Have done no lefs Diſſervice : ———

Queen. Through his Perſwaſion. ———
But, I repent, that e'er I liſten'd to him! ———
And, if he be the guilty Man, you ſay, ———

York. Your Power ſhall not protect him.

Queen. I protect him! ———
My Power! my Lords: ——— If I have any Power;
I will exert it all, to make him wretched! ———
Deliver him, to Infamy, ——— to Torture! ——— ———
May the innocent Blood of *Suffolk*, and of *Gloucefter*,
Crying aloud to Heaven, afflict his Soul!
And, everlaſting Miſery be his Portion!

And now, my Lords; ——— Henceforward, ſhall your
   Counſels
Direct My Conduct, and affiſt the King.

York. Our Counſels, Madam, if they may prevail,
Shall influence the King to rule, without You.

Salisb. You meddle, over-much, in his Affairs:
And, it were happier for the King, and Nation,
Much happier for your ſelf; would you, hereafter,
Frequent your Cloſet, more; the Council, ——— never.

Queen. Diſdainfull Men! ——— You ſlight a Friend-
   ſhip;
You tempt an Enmity; ——— diſcerning Neither. ———
You know not *Margaret!* ———

Salisb. That *England*, ne'er, had known her!

Queen. I will be known! ——— ——— Is Fortitude,
   and Wiſdom,
Given to Man, alone? ——— Prove me, in Council;
Prove me, in the Field! ——— In Policy, let *Salisbury*,
In War, let *York*, oppoſe me. ——— But, my Lords;
Be ſure, you over-match this ſlighted Woman! ———
Urge me to all Extremes! ——— Friendſhip and Fa-
   vour,

I neither ask, nor grant. —— Succefs is Mine ;
If Courage claims Succefs ! —— Yet, if We fail ;
Your Chronicles fhall witnefs to my Fame ;
Your Daughters boaft, your Sons all emulate,
A Woman's Glory ; and the World avow,
England, once, had a Queen, deferv'd to Reign !

S C E N E XV.

Salisbury.   York.

Salisb.   The daring Spirit of this Queen portends
Much Trouble to the King ; and much Difquiet,
Throughout the Land ! ——
    But ; let us to the King. —— By His Command,
My Son is gone, to pacify the People.

S C E N E. XVI.

The Lord Cardinal's Apartment.

Beaufort ; Lying on a Couch.

Why, do they lay me on a Couch of Thorns ?
How fhould I reft ! —— They bid me clofe my Eyes :
But, through the Lids, I fee a Thoufand Forms ;
Numberlefs Terrours ! —— I fhut Both Ears : And
    yet,
I hear infernal Howlings ! —— Death, and Defpair,
Have laid hold upon me. —— O, miferable, that I
    am ! ——

Would

Would I had died, as innocent, as *Gloucester!* ⸻ ⸻
Let me think no more. ⸻ ⸻ Is there no Phy-
    sician
Can cure the Mind? ⸻ Nothing, to kill Reflec-
    tion? ⸻
That I could drink Oblivion down! ⸻ O, when
Shall I have Rest! ⸻

S C E N E XVII.

Beaufort. Warwick. Eleanor.

Elean. Why, must I see the Authour of my Woes?
Warw. He cannot last, an Hour. ⸻ He raves
    on *Gloucester*;
And calls on You; imploring Your Forgiveness.
  Elean. O, hard Injunction! ⸻That we must forgive
Such Injuries! ⸻ But, ⸻ How can I forgive?
Warw. Madam, Consider his Despair! ⸻
  Elean. My Misery, my Lord! ⸻
Consider That! ⸻ I know, it is commanded: ⸻
It is a Duty: ⸻ But, ⸻ it is severe! ⸻
Warw. See, where he lies.
  Elean. Let us retire. ⸻ He sleeps. ⸻
Beauf. Who bids me sleep? ⸻ It is not safe to
    sleep! ⸻
Gloucester should not have slept. ⸻ Who are you?
    Whence? ⸻
Send away that Woman. ⸻ ⸻ Give me my
    Crown:
My Crown and Crosier! ⸻ What has the Parlia-
    ment
To do with Me? ⸻
  Elean. My Lord of *Winchester,* ⸻

                   Beauf.

Beauf. Why doeſt Thou haunt me?

Elean. Though You have made Me wretched; yet, my Lord,

I will endeavour ——

Beauf. How cameſt Thou hither? ——

Nay, then, thou art a Sorcereſs, indeed!

Can'ſt travel o'er the pathleſs Sea; can'ſt fly

In Air! —— Thou haſt bewitch'd my Senſes. ——
      Go! ——

Warw. How wild his Looks! —— Approach him not.

Beauf. Stand off! —— Let Nothing, living, come a-near me! ——

I kill, by Night! —— Alas, my feeble Age

Cannot ſupport it, longer! ——

Elean. O, ſpare him, yet, a while! ——

Warw. His Breath grows ſhort. ——

S C E N E   XVIII.

Beaufort. Warwick. Eleanor. Salisbury. York.

Salisb. How fares the Cardinal?

Warw. As one, juſt launching

Into Eternity! ——

York. Behold him, gaſping!

Beauf. Why do you ſtifle me? —— I have been at Shrift. ——

My Soul is white, as Snow! —— What needed we

Have purchas'd Votes? —— Was not the Murder cheaper?

Salisb. My Lord, the King has ſent us ——

Beauf. King of Terrours! ——

If thou beeſt Death, I'll give thee *England*'s Treaſure;

So thou wilt let me live, and feel no Pain.

York. The King my Lord, your royal Nephew, ſends ——

                                                    Beauf.

Beauf. Bring me, then, to my Trial, when you
  will. ——

Died he not in his Bed? —— Where ſhould he die? ——
Can I make Men live, whether they will, or no? ——
Alive again? —— Then, ſhew me, where he is! ——
Combe down his Hair. —— Look; look! —— It ſtands
  upright:
Like Lime-Twigs, ſet to catch my winged Soul!

Elean. Pray; pray, for Mercy! ——

Beauf. Oh, my Niece;
The Gates of Heaven are ſhut! —— —— O, ſave me;
  ſave me!
I ſhudder, on the Margin of the Gulph! ——
Headlong, I ruſh! —— I fall; deep, deep, I plunge:
I fathom Miſery; the Depths of endleſs Woe!

Elean. O, Thou eternal Mover of the Heavens;
Look, with a gentle Eye, upon this Wretch! ——
Oh, beat away the buſy, medling Fiend,
That lays ſtrong Siege to his departing Soul;
And, from his Boſome, purge this black Deſpair!

Warw. See, how the Pangs of Death work, in his
  Features!

York. Diſturb him not. —— Let him paſs, peaceably.

Elean. Lord Cardinal; —— If thou think'ſt on Hea-
  ven's Bliſs;
Hold up thy Hand: —— Make Signal of thy Hope. ——
He dies; —— and makes No Sign! —— ——

Warw. O, *Glouceſter*; —— While Thy Vertues are
  remember'd;
So long, ſhall *Beaufort*'s Infamy endure!

Elean. The tendereſt Husband! —— The moſt inhuman Uncle!

Saliſb. The Beſt, and Worſt, of Men!

Elean. Alas, my Lords;
How, ſhall I bear to live! ——

York. Be comforted. ——
With You, the Nation mourns: And *Henry*'s Sorrows
                                              Are

Are equall to your Own. —— Number'd among the
    Bleſt,
Gloucefter partakes of everlaſting Reſt. —— ——
Let high-preſuming Men with Dread attend,
Divinely warn'd, to *Beaufort*'s direfull End ! ——
Though bold Offenders human Laws defy ;
They draw down heavier Weight of Vengeance, from
    on High !

End of the Fifth A C T.

EPILOGUE.

Spoken by Mrs. *OLDFIELD.*

HE Bufinefs of an EPILOGUE, *they fay,*
Is, to deftroy the Moral of the P L A Y :
To wipe the Tears of Vertue from your Eyes ;
And make you Merry, — *left you fhould grow Wife.*

Well! — *You have heard a difmall Tale, I own :*
It, almoft, makes One dread — *to lie, alone.*
Ruffians, and Ghofts, and Murder, and Defpair,
May chace more pleafing Vifions from the Fair.
Wives can awake their Husbands, in their Fright :
But, if poor Damfels be difturb'd, by Night ;
How fhall They (helplefs Creatures !) lay the Spright ?

Forget it all ; — *And,* Beaufort's *Crime forgive :* —
Duke Humfrey *was* — *too Good a Man, to live.*
And, yet ; — *his Merit, rightly underftood ;*
We, Now, have Store of Patriots, — *full as Good !*
Great Souls ; Who, for their Countrey's Sake, would be content,
Their Spoufes fhould be doom'd — — *to Banifhment.*

Since

EPILOGUE.

Since Chronicles have drawn our Duke, so tame;
Is Eleanor, if she survives, to blame?
A Widow knows the Good, and Bad, of Life:
And, has it in her Choice, to be, or not to be, a Wife! —
Virgins, impatient, cannot stay to choose:
They risque it all; — not having Much to lose! —
I mean, —— such Nymphs, as sigh in rural Shades;
No Midnight Shepherdess, at Masquerades:
Or, such ill-fated Maids, as pine in Grotto's;
And, Never, had the Experience of Ridotto's!
Where (notwithstanding They their Market smother)
Some gain One Trinket; and, Some lose Another.

These Novelties, with Grief, considerate Women see:
For, should Italian Modes prevail; pray, What are We?
How oft' do Men our tender Spirits vex,
By telling us; We are a Trifling Sex! ——
Yet, — I am told, Philosophers maintain;
Nature makes not the smallest Thing, in vain;
And, let demurest Prudes say, What they will;
The Best of Women would be Women, still.

FINIS.